Motorbooks International Illustrated

Illustrated

Norton
BUYER'S ★ GUIDE™

Model-by-model analysis of post war singles, twins,
rotaries and specials

Roy Bacon

Niton Publishing

Published in 1991 by Niton Publishing, PO Box 3, Ventnor, Isle of Wight PO38 2AS England

British Library Cataloguing in Publication Data
Bacon, Roy H. (Roy Hunt)
  Illustrated Norton buyer's guide
  1. Norton motorcycles, history
  I. Title
629.2275
ISBN 1-85579-004-1

On the front cover: Commando Mk 3 in 1974 colour scheme and minus its electric start. Owner Richard Payne has fitted an exhaust balance pipe, reverse-cone silencers and K & N air filters. Nice one that is well used on the road and a winner at many shows and rallies.

On the back cover: The Manx Norton was one of the mainstays of the racing world for many a year, and it is seen here as shown in the 1961 brochure so near the end of its very successful days. Mike Hailwood won the Senior TT with one that year!

Filmset by Crossprint, Newport, Isle of Wight

Printed and bound in Singapore

Contents

Acknowledgements

For the third title of this series, written under the Niton Publishing imprint, I have turned to the postwar Norton machines. As with the others, it is part of a series published by Motorbooks International in the USA and Aston Publications in the UK. Thus, the three houses have combined to produce a range of Illustrated Buyer's Guides covering machines from both sides of the Atlantic.

Unlike the other two, this book was edited and type set in the UK and then printed abroad. This meant a different approach to the problems of book production and I have to thank Crossprint of the Isle of Wight for their assistance in dealing with these. They had previously helped me to get my Motorcycle Monographs off the ground so we had an established system to use, which helped.

Once again I turned to the magazines for the pictures and have to thank Peter Bolt, editor of *Motor Cycle News*, and EMAP, whose archives hold the old *Motor Cycle Weekly* files, for the bulk of them. Others came from my own archives and some I took myself, mainly at shows or museums, as will be clear from their background. A few were press pictures from the revived Norton Motors firm showing their latest machines.

The front cover picture was taken by Al Osborn at the BMF Rally of 1990 at my request and features a very nice Commando.

Some of the photographs carried the imprint of a professional and again I have to acknowledge the camera talents of G.T. Atkinson, Cecil Bailey, Reg Cave, Ken Jones, Syd Lucas, Ken Price, Publifoto, Jim Reynolds and C.E. Wardell. Some pictures came from friends Paul Adams and Art Sirota in California while one was originally sent to me by Fred Tredgett with a Classic Bike query letter. All borrowed photographs were returned to their source following publication and I have tried to make contact to clear copyright. If my letter failed to reach you or I have used an unmarked print without realising this, I can only apologise.

Finally my thanks to the professionals of the printing and book binding industry who helped me bring this title to completion.

Roy Bacon
Niton
Isle of Wight

July 1990

Introduction

The *Illustrated Norton Buyer's Guide* deals with all the postwar motorcycles right up to the modern revival of the name with the rotary-engined models. It also looks back into the past because much of the postwar design had its origins, or at least some of them, in that earlier era, and some background will help the reader to understand what came later, why, and where from.

Norton machines always commanded great respect, thanks to their many racing successes, and this continues to this day for all the models, whether single or twin and for road or track. This applies as much to the Manx racers, which still battle as hard as ever in today's classic racing, as to the Commando twins which,

Early Commando Fastback twin with kneegrips formed as part of the dualseat and nice twin-leading-shoe front brake.

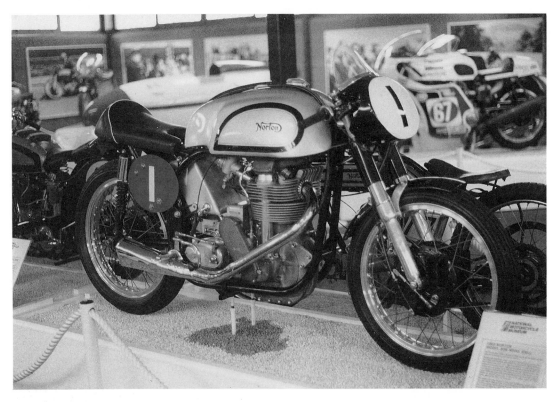

Well restored late-type Manx Norton at the National Motorcycle Museum - one of the last of the long line - valuable.

perhaps are, the most popular of those seen in regular use on the road.

Many Norton detail parts and assemblies were common to several models and years, so it is easy to construct a machine from spares and give it the correct appearance. Such work may be well done or cosmetic only but, in either case, this book will help you to make sure that you know what you are buying, as far as this is possible from an external examination.

When inspecting and buying, your weapons are the engine and frame numbers, together with the identity charts in the Appendices, plus as much information as you can find. With them, you can work out the best model for you and make sure you find it. There is more on this in the last chapter, but first we go on

a Norton model tour to see what was offered and when.

Each chapter covers a specific section of the Norton range and includes an investment rating, indicated by allocating stars from one to five. Remember that this rating is, at best, an educated guess based on conditions in 1990 and could be entirely wrong. Thus, there is no guarantee given or implied, and we can all have a good laugh about them in the next century!

Always check out current prices for your part of the world before buying, for these can be greatly affected by events. Few of us realized how the market would change during the 1980s, and over the next decade it could alter as much again in either direction.

Paul Dunstall on one of his Norton twin creations, which were highly desirable then and remain so now.

Investment rating

The investment rating system works as follows:

★★★★★ Five are the tops, the highest priced and usually have the best chance of appreciating. They are most likely to be sold by contacts and word of mouth, sometimes at auctions or, more expensively, by a specialist dealer.

★★★★ Four are the best that most people can achieve, as there are not enough five-star machines to go round. Still, they are desirable and worth having from all points of view. If advertised, check with care; one in poor condition will cost plenty to put into true four-star condition.

★★★ Three are middle-of-the-road, nice machines that hold their price along with market trends. Most machines in daily use come from this class, where good condition and reliability are the norm, but must be checked for.

★★ Two are less desirable and less likely to hold their value in the market, but can still be nice machines if they are what you want.

★ One are the machines few want, are non-original or need too much work to put right. They can be a longshot, although this is unlikely now, but as always, if it is the one you want you can probably buy it cheaply. If it is not, leave it alone.

In addition to the investment rating, a buyer must consider the three Cs - complete, correct and condition. All have a major effect on the price of the machine, but not on its ultimate star rating. First, being complete is important for a machine bought for restoration. The small details demand more attention than the large, for there are many involved in the build-up of a machine. Finding all the missing ones can be expensive and time consuming.

Second, correct parts are important for a restoration, although less so for a machine being built for daily use. The reverse applies to the third factor, condition. For the restorer is mainly concerned with having correct parts regardless, more or less, of their condition. If the machine is to be used for daily riding, then the rider will want top condition, whether the part is correct or a modern equivalent.

As always, you make your decision, pay your money and make your choice. Whatever it is, I hope it brings you good riding and much enjoyment - which just might be better than buying that five-star investment you dare not take out on the road.

Chapter 1

Forebears

Replica of the Norton twin which won its class at the first 1907 TT, with rider Rem Fowler and Bert Hopwood.

Before reviewing the Norton postwar range in detail, we have to take a look at the firm's prewar past, for much of this dictated what was done in later years. Many of the postwar models were based firmly on the older ones, while even the new twin used much from the existing range. Only the lightweight twins were to break really new ground, while the larger ones kept to their older roots right up to the late 1970s and the end of the Commando line.

Norton were a firm that kept their designs running for long periods with few changes. Their philosophy was one of steady development rather than radical alteration, so there were strong family lines which ran through the range for many years.

Much of this stemmed from the character of the founder, James Lansdowne Norton, who was a man of the highest integrity, totally honest and deeply religious. He was a skilled and innovative engineer who carried his personal standards into his work so, when he turned to motorcycles, they reflected his personality.

Early days

J.L. Norton founded his company in 1898 and produced his first motorcycle in 1902. Essentially, it was an assembly of bought-in parts and, at first, he relied on Continental engines to power his machines. It was one such, with a V-twin Peugeot engine, which won the twin-cylinder class of the first TT in 1907, but that year also heralded the first Norton single engine.

This side-valve, 634 cc single went into production in 1908 as the Big 4 model and continued as such to 1954. In all that time, the lines remained much as they were. From the start, the design provided a straight exhaust port, while the valve chamber was separated from the main part of the cylinder casting.

The rest of the machine was of the period, with direct belt drive but, already, the marque offered a good ride thanks to the long wheelbase and forward mounting of the engine. A smaller engine with bore and stroke of 79 x 100 mm followed.

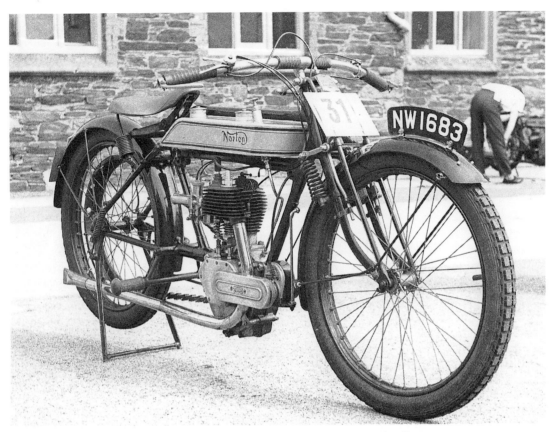

Nice early belt-drive single with side-valve engine and typical Norton engine line that was never to disappear completely.

The drive-side of a restored 1923 16H, which had all-chain drive and a three-speed gearbox.

These dimensions, and the resulting 490 cc capacity, became as well known as the marque name itself, and rightly so, for they were used up to 1963.

Further designs appeared but, as so often happens to men of ideals, Norton neglected the need to make some profit in order to stay in business and ran into financial trouble. He was taken over by R.T. Shelley, who did much of Norton's work, and production moved to a building backing on Shelley's. Later, a site in Bracebridge Street was added to provide one of the most famous of motorcycling's addresses.

Flat-tank Twenties

After the Great War, Norton kept to

Well restored 1929 model 18 with forward-mounted magneto, here with large aluminium shield to help keep the weather at bay.

their tried formula of good, solid machines - no frills and little innovation. It was to serve them well, as their reputation for building reliable models paid off in the hard times to come.

Their range was small and continued to include at least one machine with belt drive up to 1923. More exciting were the Brooklands Special, or BS, and Brooklands Road Special, or BRS, models which had tuned engines guaranteed to have exceeded 75 and 70 mph respectively at Brooklands. In fact, only the engines did this, for they were run in a slave frame at the track and classified on results. The speeds were simply minimal and failures (to reach 70 mph) were used in another, more prosaic model.

In 1922 Norton built their first overhead-valve engine by fitting a new top to the existing 490 cc lower half. The design was simple, but demonstrated a good appreciation of gas flow in the engine and cooling air flow round it. It was listed as the model 18 when it went into production, while the side-valve machines continued as the Big 4 and 16H. The last was the home version, as opposed to the 17C which had an increased ground clearance and was for 'Colonial' use.

A larger, 588 cc, ohv engine joined the 490 cc one, and a variety of specifications was offered to lengthen the range list at minimal cost. For racing, the first overhead-camshaft engine appeared in 1927 with shaft and bevel drive to the single camshaft. The 490 cc engine was designed by Walter Moore and, among its features, had the magneto mounted behind the engine where it was driven from the left-hand end of the crankshaft.

The camshaft engine went into a new cradle frame, and a similar one was fitted with the 490 cc ohv engine to create the ES2, which also had the rear-mounted magneto. Smaller, 348 cc engines with ohv and ohc joined the range, but the machines were becoming rather dated in both looks and specification as the decade came to its end.

Flat-tank Norton controls which suited the roads of the 1920s, but are less easy to live with in today's traffic.

Depressed Thirties

There were major changes to the Norton range for the new decade. A new overhead-camshaft engine, designed by Arthur Carroll, appeared in 1930 for the works machines and became a production model the next year. That year, the side and ohv singles were revised and, to all intents, took their final form.

The Carroll camshaft engine was built in 348 and 490 cc sizes and kept to shaft and bevel drive, but differed in most aspects from the Moore design. In place of the flat timing cover, running the height of the crankcase, there was a square box for the lower bevels and oil pump, chain drive from this back to the rear mounted magneto and shaft up to the cambox with its shaft and rockers.

Again, it was a design which was set to run for many years with steady develop-

ment - its essentials were still there at the end in 1963. Back in 1931 the engine drove a three-speed, handchange, gearbox and went into a rigid frame with girder forks and drum brakes.

Similar cycle parts were used for the more prosaic models, of which there were seven. Two had side-valve engines, and the rest ohv, but all had a new style of engine with dry-sump lubrication. This used a simple duplex-gear oil pump, which tended to let the oil drain into the sump when not running - nothing was done about this until 1975!

The timing cover was extended downwards to enclose the oil pump and within it went the timing gears, separate camshafts and followers. The magneto, with the dynamo strapped to its back, went behind the cylinder and was chain driven from the inlet camshaft, with a further cover to enclose this chain.

The side-valve models were the 490 cc 16H and 634 cc Big 4, while all but one of the ohv machines were of 490 cc. The exception was the 588 cc model 19 with extended stroke. The four smaller models were the 18, the 20 with twin-port head, the ES2 with cradle frame (as used by the ohc models), and the 22, which was a twin-port ES2.

From 1931 to 1939 the models gradually improved and certain features were used by all, in time, and continued in postwar years. The first of these was the Norton hub which was fitted to both wheels and most models. It could be separated into the hub itself and the brake drum, the two being held together by three sleeve nuts, so providing a quickly detachable and interchangeable feature.

Exceptions to this type were few and restricted to a one-piece front hub for the super-sporting International ohc models built for racing. The touring CS1 and CJ ohc machines kept the standard parts, but all with rear suspension had a redesigned two-part hub which was no longer quickly detachable.

All these machines had 7 in. brakes front and rear, even though the drums varied thanks to cooling ribs for the racers. All were of the single-leading-shoe design with each shoe pivoting on its own pin - very much a Norton feature for all their drum brakes from then on.

The International models, in the two engine sizes, had joined the range in 1932, and during the decade were built mainly for road racing. The touring camshaft models also continued up to 1939, but always with a slightly less glamorous specification. They were joined by the models 50 and 55 in 1933, these having 348 cc ohv engines with single or twin exhausts, and that year the 19 had its engine dimensions changed to give a 597 cc capacity.

Check springs for the front girder forks first appeared in 1933 and were used by all from 1934 on. Next on the agenda was the primary transmission, which was also altered for 1934 with a new clutch and chaincase. The clutch was a multi-plate design, with three springs and a shock absorber in its centre, while the chaincase was in pressed steel with a rubber sealing band. A single nut held the outer cover in place, and it worked well as long as the parts were not distorted or the nut tightened too far.

The next year, 1935, saw a Norton four-speed gearbox with footchange fitted to all models. This was based firmly on an older Sturmey Archer design which had been taken out of production by that firm. Norton took it over, modified it a little, and had it made for them by Burman for the next two decades.

Around 1936, a larger camshaft model of 597 cc appeared, although it was never in the lists. Few were built and all were for competition sidecar use, some for road racing and others for ISDT work. The frame for these machines had to have its top tube altered to accommodate the larger engine and was heavier than usual. The machines dominated sidecar racing until 1951 when the World Championship capacity limit was reduced to 500 cc.

Near the end of the thirties a frame with plunger rear suspension appeared, first on the ohc models and then the ES2. The side-valve and ohv engines had their valve gear enclosed, and for 1939 the Manx Grand Prix was introduced as a

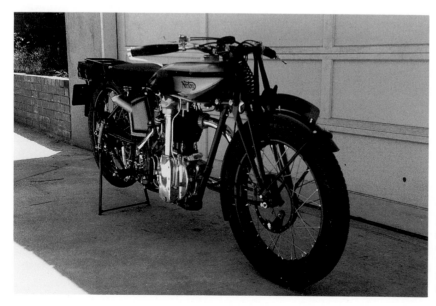

The first camshaft Norton had this style of engine, as designed by Walter Moore. This is a restored 1929 model CS1.

Norton ES2 of the 1930s at Brands Hatch in 1984. Rigid frame and girder forks combined to give excellent road holding.

pure road racer. Then came the outbreak of war, by which time Norton were already hard at work building motorcycles for the services. They had negotiated contracts well in advance, the bulk of these being for the 16H side-valve model. This was built in its 1937 form with exposed valve gear and proved to be rugged enough to withstand army use and abuse.

A smaller number of Big 4 sidecar outfits were also built for the army. These took advantage of the firm's prewar trials experience to include sidecar wheel drive in the specification. In this case, the engine design with enclosed valve gear was used, and there were minor changes incorporated for the drive shaft to the third wheel.

After the war, many 16H machines were sold off and did duty with civilians in the early postwar years when machines were in short supply and times austere. Thanks to the service use, there were large stocks of spares as well, and these proved very useful, for most fitted other models as well as the 16H.

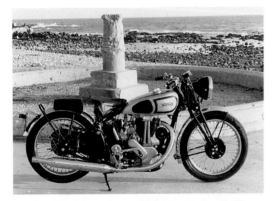

Model 18 from the late 1930s out in the Californian sunshine. Little different from the past and not to change much in the future.

On this note the firm reverted to peacetime production and entered its postwar era with two prosaic singles: the 490 cc 16 H and 18 models with side and overhead valves. Better things came later.

Chapter 2

Manx

Manx was the name used by Norton for their postwar, out-and-out, road racing models. These replaced the prewar arrangement of supplying International machines to road racing specification which had culminated, in 1939, with the Manx Grand Prix type.

Thus, the first true Manx Nortons appeared in 1946, just in time for the Manx Grand Prix races held in September of that year. In nearly all ways they were a continuation of the prewar type, but with telescopic front forks, which had been intended for the 1940 range. Internally, there was a drastic reduction in compression ratio to cope with the 72-octane pool petrol which had to be used in place of the prewar petrol-benzole mixture.

The Manx was built in two capacities as the 348 cc 40M and 498 cc 30M with common transmission and cycle parts, so the smaller model was rather overweight. The engines also had much in common, with many details the same or simply altered to suit the different bores and strokes of the two types.

The engines continued as the well established Carroll design with single overhead camshaft driven by shaft and bevel gears. They were based on a deep, vertically-split crankcase cast in magnesium alloy and ribbed externally for strength. The cases were not common to both engine sizes, but the main bearings were. These comprised a single ball race on the timing-side and both ball and roller races on the drive-side.

The bearings supported a built-up crankshaft, the mainshafts being held in the flywheels by nuts. The crankpin was in one piece, and its shoulders were pulled up against the wheels by nuts retained by locking screws. The big-end bearing itself was a double-row caged roller with the outer race pressed into the connecting rod, this being bushed at the small-end. To suit the pool petrol, the piston was flat-topped, with small valve cut-aways, and was retained on its hollow gudgeon pin by wire circlips.

The top half of the engine was all-alloy and well finned, those at the top of the barrel and all those on the head being square in plan to achieve the best cooling. The cylinder head also had a row of vertical fins above the exhaust port, which stayed as a characteristic feature to the end. The barrel had an iron sleeve for the piston to run in and its fins were symmetrical, aside from the recess on the right for the vertical shaft. Compression plates of various thickness were available to fit under it to adjust the compression ratio. As standard, this was not much more than 7:1, due to the pool petrol, but it could be raised to a more respectable 9-plus if the fuel allowed this. High-compression pistons were also listed for use with alcohol fuel.

Early postwar Manx with its plunger 'Garden Gate' frame and long Roadholder front forks.

Drive-side of a 1947 Manx with the usual left-side oil tank filler cap to suit the TT pits of that era.

Top end of the single-camshaft Manx engine and bottom edge of the scalloped petrol tank.

The cylinder head had aluminium fins cast around a bronze skull. In the best Norton tradition, the ports were direct, the inlet having a carburettor flange while the exhaust was threaded for a pipe nut. The valves were on the fore-and-aft centre-line and angled to suit the hemispherical combustion chamber, while the sparking plug lay out on the left. The complete head was held in place by four extended sleeve nuts which were fitted to long through-studs screwed into the crankcase.

The valves were controlled by pairs of hairpin springs and the lower ends of each pair were fitted into a holder. This was located on the valve guide, which was pressed in to a shoulder, and the upper holder was retained to the valve by a collar and collets. The valve springs were out in the open, which made it easy to change a broken spring, but difficult to prevent oil leaks from the valve guides.

The cambox was bolted on top of the four cylinder head sleeve nuts and was in two parts with a vertical split line. The single camshaft ran in ball races, each cam being fitted separately to the shaft and located by a peg in a system of holes. This peg also timed the top bevel gear to the shaft so that variations of valve timing could be obtained.

Each cam moved a rocker which pivoted on a double-row caged-roller bearing and whose end protruded from the cambox. This end carried the adjuster for setting the valve clearance, which was not too easy to set. This was due to the use of a taper screw with threaded sleeve which was awkward but, once set, never moved in use and would stay set for long periods.

The cambox design, unlike that of the Moore engine, was really impossible to keep oil-tight. A variety of felt pads and washers was fitted around the rocker at its pivot point, but seldom managed to keep the oil at bay for long, especially once the seals wore and took a set due to the engine heat.

The camshaft was driven by a vertical shaft which ran in a tube fitted between the top and bottom bevel housings. The shaft had Oldham couplings top and bottom which could be varied to accommodate the use, or not, of compression plates

The Amal remote needle RN carburettor with rigidly-attached float chamber, as used by the Manx in the early postwar years.

under the barrel. Each bevel housing contained a pair of bearings, for the shaft with its integral bevel gear, and was shimmed to its mounting to set the mesh of the bevel gears.

The top bevel housing was bolted to the underside of the cambox, while the lower housing was attached to the timing case housing cast as part of the right crankcase half. This box-like protrusion enclosed the right-hand end of the crankshaft which carried two gears, one a spur pinion and the other the bevel to drive the vertical shaft. The pinion meshed with a larger gear, positioned behind it, and the shaft which carried this ran in a bush fitted in the timing cover that was bolted to the housing. This cover extended back and up to the BTH magneto fitted behind the cylinder, and this instrument was chain driven from the gear shaft. An

outer cover enclosed this chain and carried the rev-counter drive gearbox, which was driven by the nut on the end of the lower sprocket shaft.

The spur gear also drove the oil pump,

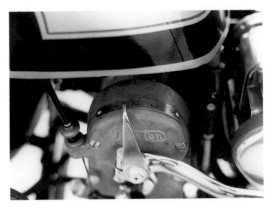

The four-speed Norton gearbox enclosed its positive-stop mechanism in an extension of the end casting.

One corner of a Manx tank, showing the bolt-through fixing used to hold it down and protect it from vibration.

but via a coupling. The pump was a duplex-gear type, to suit the dry-sump lubrication system, and the body was circular to fit in a recess in the crankcase within the timing housing. The lubricant was carried in a one-gallon oil tank of the wrap-around type. This meant that it was made to fit around the frame seat tube, rather than just to one side as those for the road models. Thus, the tank had rather poor mechanical strength, but plenty of surface area for cooling. Its wing-nut filler cap went on an extended neck on the left and was positioned to suit the TT pits of the time.

The complete engine was typically Norton, being massive, strong, rather heavy, but reliable. Its mixture was supplied by an Amal RN carburettor which was bolted to the cylinder head. This carburettor was the type with the needle hung from the side of the slide. The bottom-feed float chamber was rigidly attached to the mixing chamber, as was usual at the time. On the exhaust side, there was simply a pipe, held to the port

by a finned ring nut, and plain megaphone fitted low down on the right.

The transmission was the same as before the war, with chain primary and final drives, dry clutch out in the open and close-ratio four-speed gearbox with footchange. The gearbox was much as that used by the road models, but with revised shafts and gears to provide the racing ratios. There was no kickstarter, nor could one be fitted, as the layshaft first gear pinion could not accommodate the mechanism. The end cover was designed to suit this arrangement. Thus, it lacked the kickstart spindle boss and in its place had a housing for a ball race for the layshaft.

The change mechanism was as for the road machines, except for the gear lever itself, and just as in the past. The lever was fitted to the positive-stop mechanism which went into an extension of the gearbox end cover. From there, a link ran down to a quadrant lever, and inside the box shell the sector meshed with the camplate gear. The plate itself moved the

The Manx Norton of the early postwar years and little altered, but much developed, from the first of the Carroll engines.

A 1950 Manx, the final year for the old plunger frame, for the works machines were already benefiting from the Featherbed.

two selectors on their common rod in the manner used by the box throughout its life. Thus, one selector fork moved third gear on the mainshaft to select second and top, while the other shifted the layshaft second for the other two gears.

The gearbox worked very well, and this was as much due to the clutch as to its own good basic design. The clutch was a multi-plate type with three compression springs to clamp it up. The clutch drum ran on a caged roller bearing, and the centre contained a shock absorber. This was of the three-vane type with thick and thin rubber blocks to take the drive and overrun loads. The secret of the clutch was the massive mushroom at the end of the two-part pushrod, which forced the pressure plate to lift squarely to let the clutch plates free easily. The lift mechanism itself was a quick-thread worm in the box end cover with a lever for the control cable clamped to it.

A small cover went over the top run of the primary chain, which was otherwise exposed along with the sprockets and clutch. A guard was also provided for the rear chain which extended for most of the top run. Both chains were lubricated with oil from the main oil tank, which had two adjustable taps fitted to it for this purpose.

The engine and gearbox went into a frame known as the 'Garden Gate' type. This had plunger rear suspension and was of conventional construction, being built up from tubes that were pinned and brazed into forged lugs. The suspension was undamped, and each side simply comprised a rod clamped between frame lugs, a slider tube with the rear wheel spindle fork end fitted to it, compression and rebound springs on each side of the slider, and suitable covers. What damping there was came from the friction in the system, which could be affected by the fit of the rear wheel between the fork ends. It was hardly surprising that external dampers soon appeared on a number of machines.

At the front went the new Roadholder telescopic forks with hydraulic damping which had been developed during the war from the prewar, undamped type. The forks showed no great sophistication, but were well made and sturdy in the manner of the Norton firm. This gave them rigidity, and the result was an excellent fork action with good damping.

An Andre steering damper was fitted above the top fork yoke and was anchored to the frame by a curved strap. The damper knob was a round black moulding with serrations around its periphery, a spring clip engaging with these to maintain the set position.

The front wheel had a conical hub and a 21 in. rim on which was fitted a 3.00 in. section racing tyre. The hub was cast with external cooling ribs and had an iron liner for its 8 in. single-leading-shoe brake. The rear wheel had a hub with separate brake drum, as was fitted to all models with plunger rear suspension. The drum and hub were bolted together and ran on a single spindle, so there was no quickly detachable facility. The drum had external ribs and a 7 in. single-leading-shoe brake, while the hub was spoked to a 20 in. rim. The tyre sections were 3.25 and 3.50 in. for the 40M and 30M respectively.

Mudguards were fitted for both wheels, and the front one included a stay which could double as a stand. In fact, a prop stand was listed and took the form of a centre stand with short legs which was fitted to the frame beneath the gearbox. Its effect was to act as a prop to either side rather than to lift the wheels clear of the ground.

A pad was fitted to the rear mudguard behind the saddle, for there was no question of a dualseat in 1946, and a flyscreen gauze went ahead of the rider, being attached to the top of the front racing number plate. Behind it, on a fork-mounted bracket, went the rev-counter.

Eric Oliver won his first sidecar world title on a machine such as this, thanks to his extraordinary skills with three wheels.

Two more racing plates were supplied, one for each side of the rear wheel.

The machine was completed by the petrol tank which held over four gallons of fuel. It was in a very traditional Norton form, with a scalloped lower edge, this being done to increase the joint area between base and sides. It was also of the 'bolt-through' type with a vertical tube at each corner for a fixing stud with insulating rubbers and suitable nuts and washers. This arrangement held the tank down to the frame lugs and had been used by the factory racers as far back as 1934.

The petrol tank had a quick-action wing-nut filler cap with a breather outlet built into it. A small pipe was connected to this and ran down the front of the tank. There were two taps, one on each side, to supply the twin-feed float chamber. Both were of the taper-cock type and fitted near the rear of the tank. On the tank top went a chin pad which was held by short and long elastics that were clipped to the tank.

The machine was finished in black with the petrol and oil tanks in silver. Both were lined with a broad black outer stripe and thin red inner stripe just as in the past. The result was a handsome machine.

The 597 cc camshaft models continued to dominate sidecar racing in the early postwar years. Only one road version was built, for Cyril Quantrill of *Motor Cycling*, and this went into the plunger frame with telescopic front forks. There was a single dohc 597 cc engine, but this

First sight of the works Featherbed Norton was at Blandford in 1950, when Geoff Duke used this 499 cc machine to win with ease.

By 1956 the cylinder and head fins of the Manx had been extended, and this Junior model had a reverse-cone megaphone.

was for Eric Oliver and his champion-ship-winning outfit.

The Manx models had few changes for the next two years, but from then on were modified in the light of the factory racing experiences. Thus, a good number of features would first appear on the works racers and then, a year or two later, on the production Manx. Not all did, of course, for the works tried many developments which were either of limited success or too costly to incorporate in the standard models.

For these reasons, the private owner continued with the long-stroke, single-camshaft engine for some time, while the works had gone to short stroke and dohc before the war. It was 1949 before either

reached the standard models, and then only for selected riders who had their machines delivered just in time for the TT.

These faster men found that they had twin overhead camshafts in a new cambox and a revised cylinder head to carry it. The box was driven just as before, but had intermediate gears where the rockers had been, a cam with its drive gear at each end of the box, a single gear on the central shaft and an outrigger plate to support the parts. Each cam moved a pusher in a bronze bush which, in turn, opened the valve. This continued to be shut by a pair of hairpin springs. All in all, it was a complex assembly which required a good deal of skill to put to-

In the Isle of Man when full 'dustbin' streamlining was allowed on this Manx.

gether correctly.

Both petrol and oil tanks were changed to light alloy, to reduce their weight, and the oil tank mounting was altered to the through-bolt type. Alloy wheel rims were fitted as standard, and a conical rear hub with separate rear sprocket appeared. As at the front, the rear brake had a single pivot pin for its two shoes, unlike the road machines.

In 1950 the works machines went over to the Featherbed frame, but it was 1951 before this was adopted by the standard racing models. They continued as they were for 1950, but all had the dohc head, conical rear hub, alloy tanks and alloy rims.

The Featherbed frame set a new standard for road holding and one by which all others were measured for many

a year. It was an all-welded and fully duplex type with rear pivoted fork. The two main loops of tubing ran from the base of the headstock, itself a tube rather than a forging, along beneath the petrol tank, down behind the oil tank, and forward under the gearbox and engine before running up to the top of the headstock.

Thus, the tubes crossed over just behind the headstock with the down-tubes passing between the tank tubes. Cross-tubes joined the two main loops, and gusset plates in the lower rear quarter both braced the frame and provided a mounting for the rear fork pivot. The rear subframe was a simple tubular structure which was bolted in place to support the seat and the tops of the suspension units. The rear fork was also tubular and piv-

A Manx Norton sweeping through a typical Island corner, a job it is highly suited to.

was further reduced by the adoption of 19 in. wheels front and rear, while the rev-counter was tucked away behind the front racing plate and its mesh flyscreen.

Both tanks were new, for the petrol tank no longer needed a tunnel and, thus, became a simple box which sat on rubber pads on the top tubes. A strap, with a buckle at the rear, made it quick and easy to remove. The oil tank also became a box which sat on a platform above the gearbox in the centre of the frame. Its filler was at the top, just behind the petrol tank, and access was via a cut-out in the front of the seat. This also was new and of a proper racing type with small rear hump.

These new cycle parts were essentially what the Manx Norton was to use to the end of its days. There were to be changes, but most were minor, and the essential configuration remained the same from then on.

Into the new cycle parts went the dohc

oted on Silentbloc bushes.

At the front went shortened Roadholder forks carrying clip-on handlebars in place of the old single bend bolted to the top crown. The frontal area

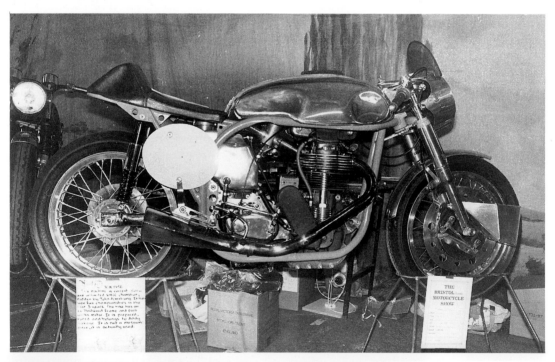

A rebuilt 1956 30M Norton which was campaigned successfully in the classic races of the 1980s.

The Manx as shown in the 1959 brochure.

engine with development changes, the most noticeable of which was a deeper crankcase with fins running down its front face and a row of four studs along its base. Less obvious was the move of the rev-counter gearbox to the left side of the cambox where it was driven by the centre shaft. This enabled a shorter cable to be used.

The gearbox was revised to suit the new installation, its shell and change mechanism being taken from the twin-cylinder model launched late in 1948. The box was known as the 'laid-down' type, as the positive-stop mechanism was moved to a position ahead of the mainshaft which gave it a more direct connection to the camplate. The move also gave a much better pedal position for the road model, but on the racer an external linkage was used, pivoting on the right footrest. Internally, the box was as before, as was the clutch and the rest of the transmission.

The two Manx models continued in this form, with a change to a GP carburet-tor for 1952. They stayed as they were for

1953, but for 1954 a good number of the works modifications were incorporated. The engines received the bulk of the changes, the main difference being a move to a shorter stroke for both so that the bore and stroke were approximately equal in both cases, the larger being 86 mm and the smaller 76 mm. The 350 alone was fitted with a reverse-cone megaphone in line with works practice.

The compression ratios were raised, thanks to the better fuel available, and the top half of the engine revised. The cylinder head was modified so that the cambox could be bolted directly to it and located on a pair of dowels. The cooling was improved with angled fins above the combustion chamber, between the valve guides, to promote air flow across the engine. These fins were augmented by the cylinder fins which were extended to encompass the vertical shaft, the head fins matching these. The top bevel housing was made integral with the head.

The cycle side was changed, the subframe being welded to the main loops. The front brake retained its 8 in. diameter

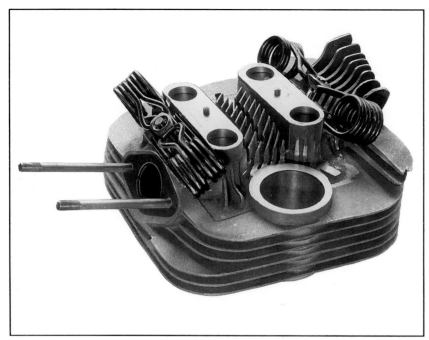

The cylinder head of the 1961 Manx to which the cambox was located on the two small dowels.

and conical hub, but became a twin-leading-shoe type with the two cams linked externally. The oil tank shape was modified to that used by the works the year before.

There were no changes for 1955, but a host of detail alterations the next year. In the bottom half of the engine, the timing-side main bearing became a flanged, double-row ball race with a higher load capacity. Its flange was secured to the crankcase by screws to prevent rotation. The top end had modified cams and a hollow, sodium-cooled, exhaust valve.

On the outside went a weir-type float chamber for the carburettor and a one-

Late-type Manx oil tank and rubber hold-down straps.

piece exhaust pipe and megaphone. The pipe was tucked up more to increase ground clearance and shorten its length, allowing the engine to rev higher. The magneto became a rotating magnet type and a magnetic rev-counter replaced the earlier model.

For the frame there were phosphor-bronze bearings in the rear fork, and the primary chain oil went into the top left-hand frame tube. Cycle side detail changes included a buffer added to help control the rear chain, the gear lever braced with a strut, welded-on lever pivots, a revised seat and no air lever. The clutch was given full disc friction rings.

This policy of detail improvement continued for 1957 when the pitch of the camshaft drive bevels was made coarser to increase the tooth strength. The inlet valve became sodium-cooled, while the big-end bearing was modified. For 1958

the gearbox was changed to what was known as the AMC type, a form adopted by the road models during 1956 and the result of the merger of Norton with the AMC group. The new gearbox retained all the essentials of the old one but had a different clutch mechanism which incorporated an adjuster in the pressure plate and dispensed with the mushroom to hold it square.

The appearance of the engine altered for 1959 when needle races were adopted for the camshaft vertical drive. They removed the need for the bottom bevel housing, the much larger shaft tube running from the crankcase housing up to the cambox. Splines in the shaft and bevels replaced the Oldham couplings of old. Both inlet and exhaust valves became solid and lost the sodium-cooling thanks to improved steels.

The Manx Norton was now nearing

On parade with a Manx. Many are now held to be too valuable to race, so are only aired on such occasions.

A 1960 Manx at a typical event of the late 1980s involving classic machines. Note 1935 International behind.

the end of its days as a production model, which showed in the long list of detail, and rather insignificant, changes introduced for 1960. While all helped in one way or another, they did little to really improve the machine. The point had been reached where power output and performance would depend more on the tuner who prepared the machine than the year it was built. Men such as Bill Lacey, Ray Petty and Steve Lancefield became as well known as the riders and machines prepared by them can still command a premium. Real proof of this expert attention must be sought, as it is all too easy to claim such ministrations.

The situation continued in this way for 1961 which was the last year the models were in the production list. They were still built for 1962, but from spares, although this did not stop further minor changes being incorporated. More significant was a new front hub with dual 7 in. brakes, each with twin-leading shoes.

That really was the end of the Manx, only a few being put together in 1963 after the works had moved from Bracebridge Street to the AMC factory in Plumstead. Not that this stopped them racing, of course, and they remained the mainstay of the 350 and 500 cc racing classes until the larger Yamaha twin took over.

In 1966 all the AMC racing hardware was sold off to Colin Seeley and, while he kept the AJS and Matchless material, he sold the Manx side to John Tickle in 1969. Tickle produced both spares and complete machines but, while these kept the Norton engine and AMC gearbox, they went into a Tickle frame to become the 350 cc T3 and 500 cc T5. Both had a high-level exhaust system which ran back at exhaust port height.

Then came a period when the Manx was overshadowed at race meetings, but did not fit into vintage racing, either. The former became the province of Yamaha and Suzuki, while the latter was either more for older machines or dominated by larger-capacity twins.

However, with the advent of classic racing the Manx was once more battling for honours on the tracks. A four-valve 500 cc engine was developed by Sid Mularney and proved, very successfully, what modern knowledge could do for the classic racing single. Finally came the classic revival of the 1980s when prices rose to unprecedented levels and few owners were keen to risk their valuable machines in the heat of racing, preferring to keep to shows and parades.

Prospects

Very good for any genuine Manx Norton, but the high prices these models command mean that great care is needed when buying. It is not too hard to cobble up something that looks like a Manx by using a road Featherbed frame, modified cycle details and an engine built up from spares or new replacement parts.

Be very wary of any claims that the machine was once owned or ridden by some well known rider or prepared by a well known tuner. Ask for complete documentary proof of all statements and accept nothing less before you part with the market price.

All Manx Nortons are a good investment and highly desirable, so the 'Garden Gate' type built up to 1950 rates four stars. The Featherbed models get five stars for all, with maybe this rating being five minus for the long-stroke type of 1951-53 and five plus for those built from 1954 on.

A marginal difference and rather dependent on whether the machine is for show or go. If the former, then condition and originality will be all important, while the latter quality can be hard to find after so many years of racing and updating. For go, a later engine is going to be better than earlier, provided it is all in very good order and correctly assembled and set up. This last will make the difference in the final run up to the flag.

The Manx T5 built by John Tickle with its high-level exhaust system and modified frame form.

★★★★	348 cc International model 40	1947-58
★★★★	490 cc International model 30	1947-58

International

The International models were introduced for the 1932 season as replicas of the works racers of the previous year and were derived from the existing CS1 and CJ machines. To this end, the International machines had more of the road racing parts and fewer of the touring, although the models were usually fitted with full electrical equipment, including lights.

This arrangement continued through the 1930s with the International machines usually being the first to receive any improvements, which would follow on the CS1 and CJ models next, and finally the side-valve and ohv singles. Not always, of course, as all went over to the new clutch and primary chaincase in 1934, and the gearbox in 1935.

However, the International models did have a four-speed footchange gearbox from the start and were fitted with the front fork check springs for 1933, a year ahead of the rest of the range. In 1935 hairpin valve springs were fitted as standard and an aluminium-bronze cylinder head offered as an option. This alloy head was meant for racing rather than road use, as the valve seats were prone to sink, so non-racers were advised to stick with the cast-iron head. For 1936 an alloy cylinder with iron liner was of-

fered as an option to go with the alloy head while, for 1938, a plunger frame also became an option.

At the end of the decade the International and touring camshaft singles were still offered, but were supplemented by the Manx Grand Prix. This was the forerunner of the postwar Manx and, like that model, was built solely for road racing. In this form, the model, in either capacity, had suitable engine internals, racing carburettor, megaphone exhaust, plunger frame and suitable gear ratios. The classic features of the type remained: the wrap-around oil tank which ran around the seat tube to fill the space normally occupied by the battery, the oil filler cap on its extended neck on the left to suit the TT pits, the scalloped petrol tank edge with the tank cut away to clear the carburettor and bolt-through fixings. On this note, the International bowed out for the duration.

After the war the model, in its two capacities, did not return to the range until 1947, when it reappeared in the more austere CS1 form while retaining the International label. Only the one pair of machines was listed, for pure racing had become the prerogative of the Manx, and for general use the overhead-valve singles were the norm.

The real job of the Inters was to contest the new Clubman's TT, first held in 1947, in which they could run without the standard silencer. It was a feature of these races that, although held for catalogue models with lights and kickstarter,

Cadwell Park supremo Charlie Wilkinson riding a 1938 International round his circuit in 1981, with helmet, but without gloves.

machines could run without electrics or silencer. Megaphones were not allowed, but the open pipe was very suited to the Inter's cams, which were designed to run without the restriction of the silencer. With it, the machine lost some 10 mph from its top speed!

The 1947 models were more akin to the prewar CS1 and CJ, for they had the all-iron engine rather than the all-alloy one. Otherwise, the engine was as before, with the ribbed crankcase containing the built-up crankshaft, shaft and bevel drive to the single camshaft, rear-mounted and chain-driven mag-dyno behind the barrel and duplex-gear oil pump. A TT carburettor supplied the mixture, and a stock tubular silencer went on the end of the exhaust pipe.

Much else of the postwar Inter was stock and taken from the ES2 model, which had the plunger rear suspension, but shared its 490 cc ohv engine with the model 18. The transmission was essentially unchanged, comprising the Norton four-speed gearbox, three-spring multi-plate clutch and pressed-steel chaincase. The one alteration was to the end covers of the gearbox, which were amended postwar to enclose the clutch worm and streamline the appearance. At first, access to the clutch cable was via a round cap, but later by means of an access cover retained by two bolts.

The frame was the stock 'Garden Gate' plunger type with minor changes to suit the camshaft engine and its petrol and oil tanks. The plunger suspension was as used by the Manx and undamped, but at the front went the Roadholder telescopic forks with their hydraulic damping. A steering damper was fitted, but was no longer the special Andre type at the top of the forks. Instead, the stock unit was mounted under the lower headrace.

The wheels used the stock hubs with their 7 in. brakes, but the tyres differed from standard, there being a 3.00 x 21 in. at the front and a 3.25 x 20 in. at the rear. The mudguards were the somewhat heavy stock parts rather than the lighter prewar type. The bulk of the detail fixtures and fittings were as used by the general range, but the tanks were special.

It was the petrol tank that gave the International models their style and line. The scallops were no more, but the shape was the same with the cut-away at the rear for the carburettor. The bolt-through fixings had also gone, so the tank had to rely on the same four bolts from under-

neath as the rest of the road range, but the overall effect made the machine.

The oil tank was just as special, for it was of the wrap-around form, but with the left-hand side abbreviated to provide room for the battery. Its filler cap went on the right, as was usual for a road machine, but the tank capacity was six pints rather than the usual four. Both tanks and the wheel rims were finished with chrome plating and black and red lining, while the petrol tank had matt silver panels - all very much in the traditional Norton manner - with the rest of the machine in black.

The International was wonderful to look at, and the larger model was to prove adequate in the Clubman's TT, but it was no road machine. It rattled, it leaked oil and the cam timing battled with the silencer to hold the road performance to around 85 mph for the 500. The 350 was slower, having to drag along virtually the same weight, within a few pounds, and thus its acceleration suffered badly.

Prewar International with plunger rear suspension and lovely large tank at a show of the 1980s.

The engine of a 1936 348 cc International with mag-dyno and driving the Norton four-speed gearbox.

Very few indeed were bought for road use in the postwar period, most being used for Clubman's racing. Occasionally, one would get a run on the road, and a good 500 could make that a memorable experience, for the engine, coupled to a close-ratio gearbox in most cases, had deep-down stamina. The plunger frame called for a firm hand and could roll at the higher speeds, but would always work with the rider to keep him out of trouble and get him through a corner.

Invariably, such machines would have been fitted with a non-standard silencer, so were best kept well away from towns. For the Clubman's TT the open pipe was even better. At the first event, in 1947, both the 350 and 500 cc races were won by International Nortons. However, both

machines were 1939 models with all-alloy engines whose extra power gave them a speed advantage, not offset too much by the girder forks. Both riders also had prewar experience of the TT course.

From then on, changes to the International models were few and far between. The close-ratio gearbox was fitted as standard from 1947 on, and in this form the model continued for the 1940s and into the 1950s. Geoff Duke won the Senior Clubman's on one in 1949, Phil Carter took the honours the next year, and Ivor Arber succeeded in 1951. However, there were no more Junior wins, for the International was too heavy and the BSA Gold Stars too fast and too numerous.

By 1951 the rear tyre section had increased to 3.50 in., but it was 1953 before

Postwar International with telescopic front forks, but retaining the plunger rear end.

there was any real change. For that year the International models took on their final form which, essentially, was that of the twin-cylinder road model with Featherbed frame, but fitted with the camshaft engine.

The 1953 Inters had all-alloy engines as standard for the first time since 1939, although there had been some so equipped in the earlier Clubman's events. Except for the change of material, the engines continued in the form they had used since 1932. Despite the passage of two decades, they still rattled and leaked oil, so they had become very dated. Compression ratios remained modest and the mixture continued to be supplied by a TT carburettor.

The engine was coupled to a laid-down gearbox, the assembly being mounted in the road-type Featherbed frame with slightly inclined rear units. The pressed-steel primary chaincase was used and short Roadholder telescopic front forks were fitted. The wheels were standard, so the tyre sizes were reduced to 3.00 x 19 in. front and 3.25 x 19 in. rear, but the front brake went up to 8 in. A seven pint oil tank went under the

dualseat nose on the right-hand side with the battery beside it.

The Inters used stock cycle parts, so the silencer became the pear-shaped type used by the rest of the range, which did nothing to unleash the performance of the engine. It was no help to the line either. Minor standard details included the underslung pilot lamp beneath the headlamp shell and the rear lamp in Diacon plastic.

The finish was the same as that of the Featherbed twin, with the painted parts in polychromatic grey. The petrol tank and wheel rims were chrome-plated with lined grey panels and centres respectively. The petrol tank was retained by a central strap, and a range of extras was listed to enable the owner to prepare the machine for the Clubman's races.

There was enough life in the old dog for Bob Keeler to win the 500 cc event, but third was the best the smaller Inter could manage among a sea of Gold Stars. It was to be the last success for the model, as time and development had overtaken it - the Gold Star was as fast, cheaper to buy, cheaper to run and much easier to work on.

Timing-side of the postwar International, which continued to fit the special large tank that gave it such style.

The Classic Bike show of 1986 and the 1949 International of L. Cooper which took the best TT machine award.

Alloy International engine in Featherbed frame, so in the model's final form.

Little else happened to the International models, although they were still listed for a while. For 1955 the subframe was welded to the main frame loops and full-width hubs were adopted for both wheels. The underslung pilot lamp went for 1956, but by then the machines were to special order only and no longer listed. They stayed as such for 1957 when they had a tubular silencer without tailpipe and revised dualseat to match the twin range.

Right at the end they had painted tanks with chrome-plated side panels, as this was the stock finish, but they remained in the grey. Some were fitted with Manx parts because these were to hand, but the laid-down gearbox seems to have been retained to the end.

The last few International machines were built in 1958, by which time they had become obsolete. They were too special and expensive at a time when any of the larger vertical twin machines was faster, simpler and readily available.

Prospects

Four stars for any International. They may have been special-purpose machines in the postwar era but they always retained their charisma and represent a sound investment. Today few owners ride them regularly due to the rattles, oil leaks and restrictions of the silencer, but all seem to love them for their apparent, and real, potential and their fine lines.

So they are a good buy and for that reason need to be checked out as carefully as a Manx. A fully documented history is an important part of this, the engine and frame numbers being only the start. Be very wary of mismatches and especially of a Featherbed Inter, as it is all too easy to install an old camshaft engine into the cycle parts of a twin or even the later ohv singles.

As with the Manx, be wary of any claims of a competition history or ownership by a known rider or dealer. Look for full documentary evidence before parting with your money and check the machine with extra care.

A variety of parts, but a nice result, using the camshaft engine to propel the assembly along.

The later International machines used the twin cycle parts to house the engine. This one needs a rear chain to complete it.

Chapter 4

Side-valve and ohv singles

★★★	490 cc	16H	1945-54
★★★	634 cc	Big 4	1947
★★★	597 cc	Big 4	1948-54
★★★	490 cc	18	1945-54
★★★	490 cc	ES2	1947-63
★	497 cc	ES2 Mk2	1965-66
★★★	597 cc	19R	1955
★★★	597 cc	19S	1955-58
★★★	348 cc	50	1956-63
★	348 cc	50 Mk2	1965-66
★★★	348 cc	Trials	1947-48
★★★	490 cc	Trials	1947-48
★★★★	490 cc	500T	1949-54

Within a week or two of World War 2 ending, a two-model Norton range, comprising the 16H and 18, was described in the motorcycle press. In some ways it picked up where it had left off six long, hard years earlier, but there was a change or two, and the firm had resisted the urge to simply continue with the wartime 16H in civilian colours.

The two machines were soon joined by the ES2 and Big 4, and the quartet of road models continued into the mid-1950s. The 16H, 18 and Big 4 were then dropped, but their places were taken by a new trio, the 19R, 19S and 50, although only the last of these survived into the 1960s along with the ES2. The Norton range of singles then came to an end, but the ES2 and 50 were briefly revived as AMC clones fitted with Norton badges.

Models suitable for competition had been part of the Norton range for many years and this practice continued after the war. The first attempt was none too successful but, from 1949, for a five year period, the firm offered the 500T, which was one of the best trials machines of the era. After 1954 there were no more competition or off-road singles but later came some twins modified for that purpose.

Road singles

The two models launched immedi-ately after the war, the 16H and 18, were both of 490 cc with the traditional Norton dimensions of 79 x 100 mm. The 16H had side valves and the 18 ohv, but in just about all other respects they were identical. Both engines were of the 1939 type with fully-enclosed valve gear, so the 16H was unlike the wartime version, which only had a cover for the valves and their springs. The bottom halves of the engines were common, except for the cam followers.

The engines were based on a cast-aluminium crankcase, split on the vertical centre-line and carrying a built-up crankshaft. There were three main bearings: a single roller race on the timing-side and roller and ball races on the drive-side. The crankshaft had its mainshafts pressed into the flywheels, with keys to locate them, and the crankpin was a tight fit in the wheels, having nuts to pull it home against shoulders.

A double row of uncaged rollers ran between the crankpin flanges and within a hardened sleeve pressed into the connecting-rod eye. A bronze bush went into the small-end and supported the fully-floating gudgeon pin, which was retained in the piston by circlips. Compression ratios were 4.9:1 for the 16H and

The ES2 had a rear-mounted magneto from the start, and its engine went into a cradle frame with triple chain stays.

6.45:1 for the 18.

Each engine had a cast-iron head and barrel, the side-valve cylinder being held down on four short studs in the crankcase. Its head sat on a gasket, was retained by a number of studs, and continued to have a screwed plug over the piston to assist in setting the ignition timing. The sparking plug was positioned over the valves, and the combustion chamber was shaped to promote good burning of the mixture.

The side-mounted valves were housed in a chest, cast as part of the barrel, but spaced away from it for good air flow. The valve chamber was sealed with a lid, held by a single nut, and within it went the valve guide and single spring for each valve, the spring being retained by a collar and collets. An exhaust valve lifter was incorporated in the chest and had an external lever to attach to the control cable.

The overhead-valve engine had long through-studs to retain both head and barrel, the latter being of a simple circular section, interrupted only by the cut-outs for the pushrod tubes. As with the side-valve engine, there was a short spigot down into the crankcase but, because of the ohv arrangement, there was also a small one into the head, plus a gasket to seal the joint.

The ohv cylinder head had a threaded exhaust port for the pipe nut, and the valves were inclined at angles to suit the combustion chamber shape. Each valve had twin coil springs which sat on a seat located on the guide and were retained by a collar and collets.

What looked like a one-piece aluminium rocker box actually comprised five details, although the design was essentially that of the one-piece type. The major part contained the rockers, each of which comprised a spindle with an arm keyed on to each end, where they were held by nuts. This housing sat on distance pieces which were shaped to match the valve wells and simply positioned the main part correctly.

The rocker housing was completed by a main cover on its right-hand side, this part having a small cover itself. The main cover and the housing were formed to clamp on to the tops of the two pushrod tubes which ran down to large attachment nuts on the top of the crankcase. The small cover gave access to the tops of the pushrods to assist in locating them to the rocker ends and for setting the valve clearances, which was done with screwed adjusters in the tops of the pushrods. A valve lifter was incorporated in the rocker box.

The valves were controlled by separate cams which went in the timing chest formed in the right-hand crankcase half. They were gear driven from the crankshaft as a train, so the drive went first to the exhaust cam gear which then meshed with the inlet gear. The inlet camshaft was extended out through the timing cover and carried a sprocket to drive the Lucas mag-dyno, which was mounted behind the cylinder. Above the cams went followers which lifted the pushrods directly for the model 18, but had tappets

A 1935 16H with sidecar out in the rain of the 1980s. A type built in large numbers during the war for the services.

The first 1947 postwar ES2, which featured the plunger rear suspension as standard along with the Roadholder front forks.

with adjusters working in guides in the crankcase for the 16H.

A duplex-gear oil pump was bolted into the timing chest beneath the crankshaft, from which it was driven by a worm wheel that was screwed on to the mainshaft to secure the timing pinion. The pump and the whole of the dry-sump lubrication system dated from 1931. However, it worked well, except for a tendency for the pump to let the oil tank contents drain through it into the sump.

The oil pump output went into the timing cover and was fed, via a pressure release valve, to the crankshaft by a spring-loaded plunger seating on its right-hand end. There was an auxiliary feed to the rear wall of the cylinder, but the valve stems of the side-valve engine and rock-

ers of the ohv one had to rely on oil mist. After it had done its job, the oil drained back to the sump where the scavenge pump returned it to the external oil tank.

A timed breather was incorporated into the crankshaft by drilling along the drive-side mainshaft to a cross-hole which aligned with a crankcase hole at the appropriate time. This hole was outboard of the outer main bearing housing on the underside, while above it there was a valve to relieve crankcase pressure.

Both engine types had a long inlet stub, which was screwed into the side-valve barrel and the ohv head. In each case it carried an Amal type 276 clip-fitting carburettor with separate float chamber. That for the 16H had a 1 in. bore, while for the model 18 it was a little

A 1947 model 18 out in California with its owner.

larger at 1-1/16 in. Both were fitted with a simple air filter.

The engines drove the stock Norton four-speed gearbox via a single-strand primary chain and multi-plate clutch just as before. The transmission was enclosed by the pressed-steel primary chaincase, and the only change was to the gearbox end covers. These were amended so that the outer enclosed the clutch worm and the cable end, but the actual operation was unaltered. Overall gearing was adjusted by using different size engine sprockets for the two models.

The engine and gearbox continued to be housed in a rigid frame with girder forks, as in prewar days, but with one difference. This was that they used the cradle frame, previously kept for the up-market camshaft and ES2 models, rather

The 16H had gained telescopic forks by 1948, but retained its rigid frame as standard to the end.

The 1947 ES2 which had so many traditional Norton features in its specification.

than the open diamond type. The front forks were the familiar Norton type with check springs, dampers and a steering damper, while the wheels had the stock offset hubs and 7 in. single-leading-shoe brakes. The rear wheel was quickly detachable, and front and rear could be interchanged, this being facilitated by both having 3.25 x 19 in. tyres.

The remainder of the machine was as before and typical of the British industry. There were ample mudguards and a saddle, beneath which was the oil tank on the right with a battery to balance it on the left. A toolbox was fitted between the right chainstays, and there were front and rear stands, a headlamp shell with ammeter and light switch, and a speedometer on the fork top that was driven by the front wheel. Finish was traditional, the petrol and oil tanks being chrome-

plated with silver panels lined in black and red, the wheel rims to match with red-lined black centres, and the rest of the painted parts in black.

Nothing was altered for 1946, but 1947 saw the introduction of the Roadholder telescopic forks and the reappearance of two further models, the ES2 and the Big 4. The forks were well constructed, featured hydraulic damping and carried the headlamp shell in lugs attached to the top shrouds. The top yoke was concealed by a panel which held the speedometer, but the ammeter and light switch stayed in the headlamp.

Of the two models making a return to the lists, the ES2 was essentially a model 18 with plunger rear suspension. This was as used by the Manx and International models so, like them, it had no damping other than that provided by the

The half-moon Norton footrest used by the firm for many years, but sadly dropped for 1957.

friction inherent in the system. In all other respects, the ES2 was as the 18, the only exception being details affected by the addition of the rear suspension.

Big 4 was a very old code that had first been used for a Norton in Edwardian days. It had been joined by a smaller version within a year, and in 1911 this took the famous 79 x 100 mm dimensions that were to be a Norton hallmark for over half a century. In time, this smaller model became the 16H, and for 1947 was expanded to produce the Big 4 once again. The revived machine had engine dimensions of 82 x 120 mm and a 634 cc capacity, just as in 1908, but in all other respects it copied the 16H, even down to the tyre size and carburettor type.

All the engines were modified for 1948, and the Big 4 dimensions were changed to 82 x 113 mm, which made the capacity 597 cc. The main alterations were to the timing chest, which was made smaller following removal of the cam followers and a switch to direct operation of the tappets by the cams. In all cases, the tappets had flat feet and, at first, were allowed to rotate. This was not totally satisfactory, so each foot had a flat added to one side to prevent rotation. Further internal changes were to smaller, but

wider, flywheels which enabled the piston skirt to be lengthened.

For the side-valve engines, the tappets extended up to the valves with adjuster screws at the top. These, and the valve springs, were enclosed in an aluminium casting shaped rather like a pair of chimney pots set side by side. The casting went between the top of the crankcase and the barrel, with seals at each end, had an access cover for the tappets, included a valve lifter and stood well clear of the cylinder wall. Engine cooling was further enhanced by the fitment of a light-alloy cylinder head to both units.

The overhead-valve engine had the same internal changes as the side-valve one, but its tappets were simply formed to match the pushrods. The rocker box was modified to a single casting, with a small access cover on the right-hand side, while the cylinder head wells were extended up to the box, removing the need

The plunger rear suspension of the postwar Norton was strong and heavy like the rest of the frame.

for the distance pieces.

The pushrod tubes went between the crankcase and rocker box, with seals at each end, and the rockers were forged in one and oscillated on fixed spindles. Valve gap adjustment continued to be at the top of the pushrods, and the rockers were lubricated from the oil return line. On the outside of the engine, the ohv machines were fitted with a silencer with the inlet and outlet in line, as used by the side-valve and International models from 1947.

Little was altered for 1949, other than the oil tank finish, which became black, but 1950 brought the laid-down gearbox which, thus, became standard for the road range with the exception of the Inters. A few of the side-valve models were built in the plunger frame, but this was never listed, even as an option, so they were rare then and rarer now. A prop stand was listed for the ES2 alone, but became common to all for 1951 when the petrol tanks were enlarged, new oil tanks fitted and the front brake backplate became a light-alloy die casting.

During 1951 the finish was amended to silver in place of chrome-plating for the petrol tank and wheel rims due to the nickel shortage. This continued, with no other changes, into 1952, but during the

Roadholder telescopic front forks and single-leading-shoe brake of the 1949 ES2.

year chrome-plating began to reappear on the wheel rims, but these had red lined, silver centres.

It was minor changes in general for 1953, except for the ES2 which adopted a new frame with pivoted-fork rear suspension. This was not, however, the Featherbed frame as, at that time, this was thought to be unsuitable for sidecar use and a number of ES2 buyers would wish to hitch chairs to their machines. Thus, the new frame was constructed

Bigger headlamp shell, but little else altered on this 1949 ES2, which was as the model 18 except for the rear suspension.

The 1954 ES2 with the bigger front brake adopted that year and the pivoted-fork frame that came in 1953 with the new silencer.

In their final 1954 year, the 16H and Big 4 gained the bigger front brake, the dualseat being a 1953 fitment. A few of each were built in the plunger frame.

A 1954 ES2 minus a kneegrip rubber, but with a headlamp beam shroud, an accessory of the period.

using traditional brazed tube-and-lug methods. It had single top, seat and downtubes. A cradle continued under the engine and gearbox and ran on to the rear subframe that supported a dualseat and the tops of the Girling rear units.

Along with the new frame came a toolbox tucked into the left-hand subframe corner with the battery ahead of it. On the right-hand side, the horn and oil tank matched these items. Further changes were to a smaller exhaust pipe and pear-shaped silencer. The petrol tank finish reverted to chrome-plating with red- and black-lined silver panels, while the wheels continued with silver centres and red lining on their chrome-plated rims.

Changes which were common to all the singles were an underslung pilot lamp and red plastic Diacon rear lamp. The rigid models adopted the dualseat as standard, despite this offering a less comfortable ride than a saddle, and the model 18 had the same tank finish as the ES2, but the side-valve machines kept to the all-silver economy finish of the previous year.

The only change for 1954 affected all models and was the fitting of an 8 in. front brake. The finish stayed as it was, and at the end of the year the two side-valve models and the ohv 18 were dropped from the range after many years of service. The market for such machines had shrunk rapidly in the early 1950s as owners moved to other types for both solo and sidecar use.

The ES2 was amended for 1955 with a light-alloy cylinder head and Amal Monobloc type 376 carburettor of 1-1/16 in. bore. This was flange mounted to the inlet tract which continued to be screwed into the head. On the cycle side there was a smaller petrol tank with round plastic badges and thinner kneegrips, a new seat, a boxed-in rear number plate and new handlebars with the horn button built into the right bar.

Sidecar owners were not forgotten, as the side-valve models were replaced by a pair of ohv machines that revived a pre-war model number. These were the 19R with rigid frame and 19S with pivoted

49

The rigid-framed model 19R, only built for 1955, which was to placate sidecar drivers for the loss of the side-valve machines.

Engine of a 1957 model 50, the 348 cc single which returned to the range for the previous year.

rear fork, both using the Big 4 597 cc capacity and 82 x 113 mm dimensions.

Except for the capacity, the 19S duplicated the ES2 down to the carburettor and tyre sizes, but it did have higher gearing. The 19R was as the model 18 in its rigid frame and kept that machine's tubular silencer, but it had lower gearing and a 4.00 x 18 in. rear tyre to suit sidecar use. It only remained in the range for one year, cynics suggesting that its real purpose was to use up the stock of rigid frames.

This left the ES2 and 19S for 1956, but they were joined by the similar model 50, it being difficult to tell all three apart. The new machine also revived a prewar model code, and its 348 cc capacity came from 71 x 88 mm dimensions. The compression ratio of the existing models was raised a little and their cylinder fin area increased. The ES2 had the same size exhaust pipe as the 19S, and both had an improved exhaust cam. The carburettors remained as they were, the model 50 being fitted

The 1955 ES2 with new light-alloy cylinder head, Monobloc carburettor and other detail changes.

with a type 376 of 1 in. bore.

All three singles shared common cycle parts which had a good number of changes. The first of these were full-width light-alloy hubs for both wheels, but with the same brakes as in the past. The front forks had softer springs and the speedometer panel at the top was dropped. To accommodate the instrument, the headlamp shell was made deeper and its panel increased in size to carry the speedometer as well as the ammeter and light switch. The pilot lamp was moved to the main reflector, so the underslung light was no more, and the dipswitch and horn button were combined on the left bar.

There was a new oil tank with ribs which filled the whole of the right-hand subframe corner and was matched on the left by a combined tool and battery box, which also housed the dynamo regulator. The air cleaner went between the two and was connected to the carburettor by hose. The dualseat was new with a flat

top, and there were new mudguards, an improved prop stand and a change to Armstrong rear units. The petrol tank increased in size once more.

Towards the end of the model year, the gearbox was changed to what became known as the AMC type. Norton had merged into the AMC group in 1953, and the intention was to use their extensive gear cutting facilities to make gearboxes for the group. Thus, the gearbox went on AJS and Matchless singles and twins as well as the Norton machines, although there could be minor variations in the shell lugs or mainshaft features.

The AMC gearbox was to continue in use up to 1977 on some Norton twins, and the bulk of it was really no different from the laid-down type or the original prewar design that preceded it. What was changed was the positive-stop mechanism, which became smaller and neater, but in the end moved a round camplate as in the past. It did permit the use of more compact end covers, how-

The singles for 1957 came in three capacities, all with a new cylinder head, revised frame and AMC gearbox.

ever.

The other major alteration to the gearbox was the clutch lift mechanism. This became a shaped arm which moved the pushrod. Unfortunately, this design required an adjuster in the centre of the pressure plate, so there was no longer a clutch mushroom to help hold the plate square. This became dependent on careful adjustment of the springs.

All three singles had a new cylinder head for 1957. This included a flange for the carburettor and integral pushrod tunnels. Thus, the pushrod tubes went into the underside of the head and continued to seal to the top of the crankcase.

For 1958 there were no changes for the singles, but this model 19S was dropped at the end of the year.

The change to alternator electrics and coil ignition for 1959 brought this points housing in the old magneto position.

There were new cams within the timing chest with extended quietening ramps and a little more lift.

On the cycle side, the frame cradle casting went, so the lower tubes ran forward to the bottom of the downtube, and the rear suspension units changed back to Girlings. There were a host of detail alterations which included a new front hub and backplate, instruments mounted directly in the headlamp shell rather than on a separate panel, a tubular silencer with no tailpipe, and a revision to the finish. This continued in black, but the petrol tank was amended to matt silver all over with separate chrome-plated side panels, round plastic badges and kneegrips.

There were no changes to specification or finish for 1958, and at the end of

Both ohv singles adopted the Featherbed frame for 1959, and this ES2 has the optional full rear chaincase fitted.

For 1961 the sin-
gles used the
slimline Feather-
bed frame with a
new petrol tank as
on this ES2.

that season the 19S was dropped from the range. Its job had been taken over by the twins which, by now, were dominating the firm's production, although their fame remained closely allied to the racing Manx.

Both engine and frame were notice-ably altered for 1959 when the first went over to alternator electrics and coil igni-tion, while the cycle side adopted the Featherbed frame. The changes were accentuated by a Forest green finish for

Drive-side of the 1961 ES2 with its alternator within the familiar pressed-steel primary chaincase.

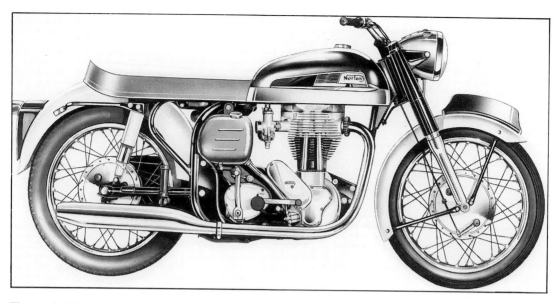

The model 50 of 1961 was very similar to the larger ES2 which made it overweight and over-braked for its power.

all painted parts of both models, although the more traditional black and silver remained an option in its 1957 form.

The Lucas RM15 alternator was mounted within the primary chaincase, whose outer was amended to clear the stator bolted to the crankcase. Output control was effected by switching coils into circuit using the light switch, and a rectifier converted the current to direct form. The coil ignition was controlled by points housed, with an auto-advance, in an assembly which replaced the magneto, but kept the chain to drive it.

The Featherbed frame that housed the engine and gearbox was essentially that used by the twins. The engine plates were amended to suit, and shortened Roadholder forks went at the front. These were available with special yokes to suit sidecar use, along with heavy-duty springs to cope with the added load. The tyre sizes were amended to 3.00 x 19 in. front and 3.50 x 19 in. rear, while the petrol tank capacity went back to 3 gallons. A full rear chaincase was added to

the option list.

After all these alterations, it was hardly surprising that little changed for 1960. The internal gearbox ratios were altered, this being general to the range, and chrome-plated mudguards became an option.

The 1961 changes were major in that they brought in a new frame and two-tone finish for the singles, but had little real effect on how the machines performed. The frame became the type known as the 'slimline', which had been introduced the year before for the twins to suit their rear enclosure. The change was made by pulling in the upper rear main loop corners to reduce the width in the vicinity of the dualseat nose, and the seat was narrowed to match. Inevitably, the old Featherbed frame became the 'wideline'.

The petrol tank was slimmer, but held a little more fuel, while on its sides went new badges running most of its length. They incorporated small kneegrips at the rear and acted as the break between the

A nicely restored model 50 seen in later years and featuring the two-tone finish used from then on.

two tank colours. Thus, the finish was quite different from the traditional Norton of old, although much of the model 50 was in black. This included the upper petrol tank, but the lower tank and mudguards were in dove grey, as they were for the ES2. The remainder of that machine was in green, and both models continued with the option of chrome-plated mudguards.

There was no change to the finish for 1962, and only the fitting of the higher-output RM19 alternator affected the specification. Only the finish was altered for 1963 when the two-tone colours became black and off-white for both models, the latter colour replacing grey for the lower tank and mudguards.

At the end of 1963 the long line of faithful singles finally came to an end, for

they had no real place in the motorcycle world. Fashion and legislation had produced a two-model market: a hot 250, for learners restricted to that capacity, and a big twin for those riders who had passed their driving test. Norton production had been transferred from its traditional Bracebridge Street home in Birmingham to the AMC works in Plumstead at the end of 1962, so the last machines were built in South London. The group was beginning to run into financial trouble, and as a result there were some desperate combinations of AMC and Norton parts to produce hybrids.

Most of the hybrids were twins, but both the ES2 and model 50 were built in Mk 2 forms for 1965, using AMC parts. Effectively, they were the AJS model 16 and 18, or Matchless G3 and G80, of 348

Some owners prefer the traditional Norton black and silver finish for any machine, whether single or twin

and 497 cc respectively. These used the Norton Roadholder forks and full-width light-alloy hubs in their AMC form, and they became Nortons by the simple expedient of fitting Norton badges to the petrol tank. This did nothing to endear any of the machines to any of the marque's enthusiasts.

The two models ran on into 1966 with minor tank styling changes, but then they were discontinued, having made no impact at all on the market. So ended the Norton singles line.

Prospects

Generally middle of the road and quite good, except for the AMC clones which are only worth one star each - they might even be worth more if turned into an AJS or Matchless with a switch of badges. For the rest, I would award three stars, al-

though this could vary plus or minus a half, depending on the model.

The ohv models would be plus, the side-valves a minus, while the plunger ES2 rates above the rigid model 18. Any side-valve model in a plunger frame is rare so is a plus and possibly worth four stars, but only just! The rigid 19R is another rare one so is worth as much or more than the sprung version, as long as it is genuine. Be wary of a model 18 or 16H with a 19 engine installed.

Featherbed singles are as desirable as plunger or rigid ones and offer impeccable handling without too much of the hard ride of the earlier models. All the singles tend to have hard rather than soft suspension, but they hold their line well when cornering. Brakes, especially the 8 in. front, should be quite adequate for the power, the model 50 perhaps being the

Really a hybrid with AMC engine and frame, group gearbox and Norton forks and wheels. Did not sell with AMC badge on it either.

most over-specified machine of all time in terms of brakes and handling. It could even have a twin-leading-shoe backplate installed, but nothing much can be done to improve its slow acceleration, which is due to the weight it has to pull along.

The Norton singles are not really about flashing acceleration and high speed, for they were built for a pre-motorway age. The heavy flywheels, relatively small carburettor and mild cam timings all worked together to produce low-down torque and pulling power. The machines were able to carry riders in a relaxed manner at a respectable average, for they were little troubled by hills and ran round the bends with no need to slow down. On the roads of the times, they covered ground at a faster gait than was apparent and without the rider having to work hard to achieve this.

The machines, especially the ohv models, offer a particular form of motor-cycling which has a great deal of charm and they do this very well. Thus, while they may not be the investment an International can be, they can offer a nice way to enjoy two wheels.

Trials models

Norton were building machines for off-road use as far back as 1921, but for many years this simply amounted to what was known as a 'Colonial' specification.

Very desirable trials 500T in its final year. Only built from 1949 to 1954 and little altered over that time.

For this, they used a frame which increased the ground clearance and raised the exhaust system, but little else was altered. The 'Colonial' model with its 490 cc side-valve engine was, at first, simply another version of the model 16, but for 1921 it became the 17C, while the home market model with stock lower frame took the famous 16H code. By the late 1920s the 17C was no longer listed, but the 16H ran on to 1954.

From the mid-1930s the firm offered any model to a trials specification. This provided competition tyres, an upswept exhaust and narrow mudguards. This still left the result rather long and heavy, but it was accepted by the riders of that time and was common practice. Some of the works men used the camshaft engine, especially for six-days events, and, if they had the chance, the sidecar drivers opted for the larger 597 cc camshaft engine. This was built in small numbers in the late 1930s for trials work and sidecar racing.

After the war, Norton produced a few machines in the same manner, and these were listed as the 350 Trials and 500 Trials. They were totally unsuitable, even

for the events of the day, for they were based on the model 18 with little alteration. No road 350 existed at the time, but no doubt prewar model 50 spares enabled a few engines to be built, as so much was common with the model 18.

The machines came with a 21 in. front wheel, competition tyres, Roadholder forks and full electrics, but did have a raised exhaust system and narrow-section mudguards, although the front one remained unsprung and close fitting. Private owners, who were few in number, fitted girder forks which reduced the wheelbase and cut down some of the weight, but the result was still barely acceptable and was more of a trail machine than a trials mount. Works riders had to make the best of it, and did, as works riders always managed to do.

During 1948 the works team had something rather better, courtesy of the McCandless brothers, who were better known for their later work in designing the Featherbed frame. For the trials world they took most of the parts they needed from the Norton parts list, added a few modified ones, and the result was the 500T, a classic of its day.

The 500T used the main frame from the wartime 16H, as this gave more ground clearance, and had a sump plate added to protect the front and underside of the crankcase. The rear frame was short and barely allowed the gearbox to be squeezed in between the seat tube and the rear wheel, but it was the fork yokes that played the main part in reducing the wheelbase.

The yokes were altered so that they held the Roadholder fork legs much further to the rear than usual. For the prototype, this was done by cutting and welding. To enable the forks to have a good lock, essential for trials, a slim, steel, 2 gallon petrol tank was used. The tank was mounted on two horizontal prongs, with rubber insulation, at the front, and was held down on rubber by a single fixing at the rear, so it was easy to remove.

The engine fitted into the prototypes was the standard 490 cc ohv, as used by the model 18 and ES2, but with the compression ratio reduced a little. In production, it had an alloy top half, continued with the same carburettor size, and kept the stock primary transmission and chaincase to drive the four-speed gearbox. This was fitted with a set of wide-ratio gears, the overall ratio being lowered to suit the use. It retained the pre-war end covers, but these were modified to tuck the kickstarter boss in more than usual. Thus, the clutch worm and cable end were exposed to the weather and generally muddy conditions of trials events.

The rear hub was stock and spoked into a wheel fitted with a high-tensile steel rim and 4.00 x 19 in. tyre. The front rim was also of high-tensile steel and carried a 2.75 x 21 in. tyre, but the hub had a scalloped brake-side flange and light-alloy brake backplate with ribs to support the cam spindle boss. Both mudguards were narrow and in light-alloy,

but painted black.

A 16H oil tank was used with a minor change to a vertical filler neck, the rider sat on a Dunlop trials saddle, and a toolbox went on the right-hand side above the upper chainstay. The exhaust pipe ran low down on the right and back to a slightly tilted tubular silencer. There was a tucked-in prop stand as well as the rear one, the latter usually being quickly discarded by riders. The speedometer went into a Manx rev-counter mounting, so it was tucked into the top yoke very neatly.

There was talk of an optional lighting set with a quickly detachable headlamp which attached to the wire harness with a plug and socket. Presumably, the fitting of this set would have meant a change from the standard BTH magneto, with its excellent low-speed sparking, to a Lucas mag-dyno. In fact, nothing is shown for the 500T in the Lucas works list, which supports the view that the lighting set was only ever a thought.

Finish was mainly black, the tank being dull chrome-plated with a silver top panel lined in red and black, and very handsome it was. The model was an immediate success and found favour with the trials riders of the day. The engine was a tight fit in the frame, and it was none too easy to keep a gas-tight joint between head and barrel. However, the heavy flywheels drove the machine through sections well.

Some 500T machines were used in scrambles, and others had a trials sidecar hitched to them, but the model coped well enough with either circumstance. Various light-alloy parts appeared on the works models, all copied without too much trouble by private owners, and some engines were extended to 600 cc. This involved flywheels from the Big 4 or 19 and a spacer under the cylinder but, again, was not difficult to arrange.

From then on, the 500T had little alteration in its five-year life. Bottom gear was raised in the box for 1950, and the front hub scallops went for 1951, while the rear brake backplate copied the front with a change to light-alloy for its material. Nothing was altered for 1952, but it was reported that a die-cast head was fitted for 1953, and the quoted power output went up a little.

It was suggested that a Lucas magneto was fitted for 1954, but this is not supported by the Lucas lists and seems to come from the general nature of the specification in the brochure. This also indicates the fitment of the 8 in. brake adopted by the road models that year, but this is unlikely for a trials model. Examples do exist, but more likely arise from a demand made by the original buyer of the machine or a later change.

On that note, the 500T was dropped from the range after its five years of service, during which it remained virtually unaltered. This simplified the supply of spares, which was made even easier by the fact that so many items were common to other machines in the range. It was never fitted with the laid-down gearbox, as there was simply no room to get this in. There was talk of a 348 cc version, but this never appeared in the range, although it is possible that the Norton competition shop built one or two to contest that capacity.

Prospects

Three stars for the 350 and 500 Trials models because they are so rare and awful, but they do not constitute a collector's machine in any other way. Because they are rare, they should hold up as well as any other, but as machines to use they rank low. It is unlikely that any actually remain, for there would have been no point in keeping them in the trials format.

The 500T is completely different and worth four stars of anyone's money. Plus four rather than minus four, especially if in original form and finish. Nice to have and nice to ride in pre-65 events where it can hold its own, for it was always as good as, or better than, its contemporaries.

It is a model to check out with care to make sure it is as genuine as may be claimed. For trials use, it must have the right fork yokes, and equally essentially is an unworn carburettor so that a flick of the throttle wrist can pick up the front wheel.

Chapter 5

Dominator & Featherbed twins

★★★	497 cc	7	1949-55
★★★★	497 cc	88	1952-63
★★★★	497 cc	88 dl	1960-62
★★★★	497 cc	88SS	1961-66
★★★★	596 cc	99	1956-62
★★★★	596 cc	99 dl	1960-62
★★★★	596 cc	99SS	1961-62
★★★	596 cc	77	1957-58
★★★★	646 cc	650	1961-63
★★★★	646 cc	650 dl	1962
★★★★	646 cc	650SS	1962-68
★★★★	646 cc	Mercury	1969-70
★★★★	745 cc	Atlas	1962-68

Up to the late 1940s, Norton were known for their single-cylinder machines, and it was only with effort that one recalled that their first TT success had been with a twin back in 1907. They ceased to use twin cylinders soon after that date, and it was after World War 2 before they turned their attention to them again.

In this, along with the other major British firms, they were forced to follow the lead set by Triumph with their 1938 Speed Twin. This was so successful that no firm could be without one so, first BSA, and later Ariel, AMC, Royal Enfield and Norton, followed suit with their individual designs.

Norton's first postwar twin was designed by Jack Moore and followed the lines of the Triumph quite closely. It was only ever built as a mock-up, using ES2 parts, and when Bert Hopwood joined Norton early in 1947 the Moore twin was forgotten. Hopwood's task was to design a twin-cylinder engine for Norton. While laying this out, he reflected on his experience of the Triumph engine and worked to avoid its problems. In this he was sufficiently successful for the basic engine to continue in production for some 30 years.

Dominator Model 7

The complete machine was launched at Earls Court in November 1948 as the Model 7 or Dominator, and while the cycle side was mainly ES2, but with the laid-down gearbox, the engine was brand new. The basic pattern of the engine was the same as the other British vertical twins with a 360 degree crankshaft. This gave the machine a nice even exhaust note, always an important facet with owners, and allowed the use of a standard twin-cylinder magneto and single carburettor.

The engine was mounted with its cylinders vertical. Their dimensions were 66 x 72.6 mm, so the capacity came out at 497 cc. Its construction was based on a cast-aluminium crankcase split vertically on the engine centre-line. Each case half carried a single main bearing of the same size, but that on the drive-side was a roller race, while the timing-side had a ball race. There was an oil seal outboard of the roller race and a sealing disc by the timing-side bearing.

The crankshaft had a central cast-iron flywheel clamped between two half-cranks so it was built up with studs and bolts to hold it together. Thus, a sludge trap was formed within the flywheel, and the crankpins were hollow and part of the oil-feed system to the big-ends. Light-alloy connecting rods with shell bearings were used and had bronze bushes at the small-ends for the gudgeon pins. The three-ring pistons had flat tops, were handed by their valve cut-aways and gave a 6.7:1 compression ratio.

A one-piece, cast-iron cylinder block sat on the crankcase, to which it was secured by an array of studs. There were pushrod tunnels at the front, being spaced away from the main casting to assist air flow and cooling. The tappets were fitted in holes at the bases of the tunnels where they were retained by a keeper, which also prevented them from rotating.

The cylinder head was a one-piece iron casting with integral rocker box and into which the block was spigoted with a copper-asbestos gasket to seal the joint. The fixings between head and block were designed to have a minimal effect on the cooling air flow, and while this arrange-ment worked well, it did not make them easy to remove or replace. The exhaust ports were widely splayed and threaded for pipe nuts, while the inlet manifold was originally cast as part of the head. This was quickly changed for a separate aluminium manifold which was bolted to the head and carried an Amal Type 276 carburettor of 1 in. bore with separate float chamber.

The combustion chamber shape and narrow valve angle added up to an excel-lent design which was to run on for many years. The detail parts within it were conventional, duplex valve springs be-ing seated on a cup located on each valve guide and retained by a collar and collets. The rockers were forgings and each oscil-lated on a fixed pin, these pins being splayed round to match the exhaust ports.

Dominator model 7 twin in its first form with the plunger frame and long Roadholder forks. Nice period extras on this one.

Engine unit of the early model 7 with iron head and block, single carburettor and forward camshaft location.

At first, each pin was formed with an end plate, but this was soon altered to separate parts which sealed the pin and prevented it rotating. Valve gaps were set by adjusters at the outer rocker ends, and the access to these was enclosed by one cover for each exhaust and a single cover for the inlet.

The camshaft ran across the front of the engine in bronze bushes high up in the crankcase, so it was directly beneath the tappets in the block. A timed breather was driven by the left-hand end of the camshaft which was itself rotated by gear and chain from the crankshaft's right-hand end. The first stage in this was from a crankshaft pinion to an intermediate gear that ran on a spindle pressed into the crankcase wall. This gear ran at half engine speed and incorporated two chain sprockets, one being connected to the camshaft by chain and tensioned with a slipper.

The second sprocket, which was part of the intermediate gear, drove a Lucas K2F magneto that was flange-mounted to the back of the timing chest behind the cylinder block. The three mounting studs allowed the magneto to move enough to set the chain tension, and an auto-advance was built into the magneto sprocket.

The Lucas dynamo was clamped to the front of the crankcase and took its drive from the camshaft sprocket, this sprocket being combined with a large fibre gear which it drove via a slipping clutch. The fibre gear mated with a small pinion on the dynamo armature, which extended into the timing chest to do this. The hole in the timing chest wall was large enough to allow the pinion to pass through it so the dynamo could readily be removed.

The lubrication system was based on the Norton duplex-gear oil pump, and this went in the timing chest beneath the crankshaft, which drove it by worm nut, as was usual for the marque. The whole of the drive system to camshaft, magneto, dynamo and oil pump was enclosed by a single timing cover. This cover carried a pressure release valve for the oil system and was fitted with an oil seal which ran on the extreme right-hand crankshaft end. This ensured that the oil supply went into the mainshaft and, thus, reached the big-ends. A connection from the pressure side of the system ran up to an oil gauge set in the top of the petrol tank, but the oil for the rocker box was taken from the return line running from the crankcase to the external oil tank.

From that point on, the Dominator was a copy of the ES2, but with the laid-down gearbox from the start. Thus, there was a single-strand primary chain, multi-plate clutch, four speeds and the pressed-steel primary chaincase. The mechanical parts went into the cradle frame with plunger rear suspension and the Roadholder telescopic forks at the front. A version with a rigid frame was projected for sidecar owners, and there was an alloy cylinder and block shown in the original brochure as an option, but neither came to anything.

The Model 7 had the usual Norton wheels with offset hubs and 7 in. brakes. At the front the tyre size was 3.00 x 21 in., while for the rear it was 3.50 x 19 in., the speedometer drive being taken from the hub. For the rest, it was touring mud-guards, saddle, oil tank, toolbox, centre stand and a low-level exhaust pipe and silencer on each side of the machine. The speedometer went into a fork-top panel, and the ammeter and light switch in a panel fixed to the headlamp shell. A horn hung from a saddle lug, just aft of the battery on the left-hand side, the controls were conventional, and the finish mainly black. This was relieved by having the petrol tank chrome-plated with silver panels, lined in red and black, while the wheel rims were plated with black centres lined in red. For press and show models, the centres were often in silver, which can confuse, for it was these machines that were most often photographed for magazines.

Most Dominator machines went for export at first, but a few reached the home market where they proved popular. There were no changes for 1950, although a few export machines went out with blue or red tank panels. For 1951, there was only a revision to the front brake. The size stayed as it was, but the original one-piece hub was altered to a cast-iron drum riveted to the hub, while the backplate became a light-alloy casting.

The 1952 finish was austere, due to a nickel shortage, so the petrol tank was in silver with red and black to outline the panels. The wheel rim centre colour be-

By 1955 the model 7 had a light-alloy cylinder head, pear-shaped silencers and a pivoted-fork frame.

The Featherbed model 88 twin for 1954 with bigger front brake and leaner mudguard, but still with the iron cylinder head.

came silver as standard during the year, but otherwise the Dominator remained as before.

Not so for 1953 when the engine and gearbox went into a new frame with pivoted-fork rear suspension. This was much as that used by the ES2 single, but with Armstrong rear units. With the new frame came the pear-shaped silencers, dualseat and underslung pilot lamp, while the front tyre was reduced in size to 3.25 x 19 in. The tank-mounted oil gauge was no longer fitted, and the finish was unchanged.

The only alteration for 1954 was to an 8 in. front brake, but the finish reverted to its former style with chrome-plating for the tank and rims. There were more changes for 1955, as the cylinder-head material became light-alloy, a Monobloc carburettor was fitted (although the size remained the same), and there were new round tank badges, moulded in plastic. The rear number plate was boxed in, and

The laid-down gearbox as used by the twins from the start, but derived from the older type.

Norton pressed-steel
primary chaincase,
as first seen in 1934
and here on a 1953
model 88 twin.

the dualseat was new and more shapely than the earlier slab-like version.

At the end of 1955 the Dominator Model 7 was dropped, as the firm concentrated on the Featherbed twin which was much more popular.

Prospects

Model 7 twins are now rare, but are still less valued than the better known Featherbed machines. They are nice machines to ride but, with an all-iron engine and early carburettor, except for the last year, are not to everyone's taste.

So, they get three stars for a middle-of-the-road four-stroke. Good, solid stars, of course, but no more than that. Possibly the plunger model is a better investment than the pivoted-fork version because it relates to an earlier age of Norton history. In either case, be wary of hybrids built up using later engines or single-cylinder frames. Check those numbers, including the essential prefixes and year letter!

Featherbed twin

The Norton twin with Featherbed frame was officially known as the Model

88 Dominator de-luxe at first, but soon took the frame name as the model title. In time, when other versions and capacities joined the original, all were known simply by their model number with a suitable suffix to indicate their build style.

As soon as the Manx became available with the Featherbed frame, customers began to clamour for a road twin in the same form, and a foretaste of this was seen at Assen when the Dutch Grand Prix was run there during 1951. Another was spotted during selection trials for the ISDT that year, albeit with Manx front brake and many detail changes to suit its use.

The Model 88 was launched late that year for the 1952 season and was a success from the start. So much so, that all production went for export at first, and home buyers could only look and long.

The new model had a production version of the racing frame, made using a commercial grade of steel tubing. The subframe was bolted to the main section, and the rear fork was pivoted on Silentbloc bushes and controlled by hydraulically-damped spring units. Shortened Roadholder forks, similar to the Manx

The fork-top panel used by the early model 88 twins for the two instruments and the light switch.

type, went at the front, angular-contact ball bearings being fitted to support them in the headstock. Internal fork springs were used, but there was no steering damper.

Engine plates held the standard Model 7 engine and gearbox as a single assembly in the frame, and the primary transmission was enclosed by a stock chaincase. The rest of the machine differed in many ways. The front mudguard was sprung and deeply valanced,

Well restored 1956 model 99, the first year of the 596 cc twin and the first enlargement of the original engine.

The short-lived model 77, which used the 596 cc engine in the model 7 cycle parts to create a machine for the sidecar market.

which made the front end of the machine seem a little heavy, and a panel at the top of the forks held the speedometer, ammeter and light switch. From the start there was an underslung pilot lamp, pear-

shaped silencers, a nice dualseat held by two thumb-screws, and a tooltray beneath the seat.

Both the oil tank and battery were in their usual places, but mounted on a plat-

Model 99 for 1957 with revised tank finish and AMC gearbox. The full-width, light-alloy hubs had been adopted from 1955.

Rear enclosure was introduced to follow a trend and produced the de luxe series, this being a 1960 99 model.

form above the gearbox rather than from the frame, and the petrol tank was held down by a top strap and seated on rubber pads on the frame top-tubes. The wheel hubs were common with the Model 7, as was the rear tyre size, but at the front, the Model 88 had a 3.25 x 19 in. tyre.

Finish for the Model 88 was mainly in grey with, at first, a black frame, which was soon altered to match the rest of the machine. The petrol tank was chrome-plated with grey panels lined in red and black, while the wheel rims matched with grey centres, lined red, on chrome-plating. During 1952 the rim centre colour changed to silver and some export machines went out with blue tank panels.

For 1953 the Model 88 was fitted with a much lighter, unsprung, front mud-guard, Armstrong rear suspension units and a 3.00 in. section front tyre. The finish was not changed, but an option in the traditional Norton black and silver was listed. The front brake size was increased to 8 in. for 1954, but otherwise the machine stayed as it was.

Much more happened for 1955 when the engine was fitted with the light-alloy cylinder head and supplied by a Monobloc carburettor. On the cycle side, the subframe was welded to the main loops (instead of being bolted in place), there were full-width, light-alloy hubs for both wheels with the hubs ribbed for strength and cooling, and a new dualseat. The rear number plate was boxed in, and round plastic badges appeared on the sides of the petrol tank to enhance the looks, while the finish remained in grey with chrome-plating.

The removal of the Model 7 from the list for 1956 allowed the firm to concentrate on the more popular Featherbed twin, and for that year it was joined by a larger version. This was the Model 99 whose engine was stretched out to 596 cc, with 68 x 82 mm dimensions, and fitted with a 1-1/16 in. Monobloc. The compression ratio of the larger engine was 7.4:1, while that of the smaller was raised to 7.8:1.

The Model 99 had higher gearing than the Model 88, but in other respects the two were the same, albeit amended from

The 646 cc model was introduced for 1961 as the Manxman and was available on the USA market only at first.

the previous year. For 1956 there was a new oil tank, which was matched by a battery box on the left-hand side of the machine. The underslung pilot lamp went, as did the fork-top panel, and the headlamp shell was made deeper to accommodate the speedometer, ammeter and light switch on a detachable panel. There was no change to the finish except

A de luxe version of the 650 was listed for 1962 only and followed the lines of the other two capacities.

for the addition of a miniature tank badge in the timing cover.

In May 1956 the twins went over to the AMC gearbox, and for 1957 were fitted with tubular silencers without tailpipes. Minor alterations included plain round footrests in place of the old-style Norton half-moon section and increased finning between the exhaust ports of the cylinder head. The front brake drum was cast in place instead of being bolted, and there was no panel in the headlamp shell, so the detail items were directly mounted. Girling units began to replace the Armstrong ones and, while the finish remained in grey, the petrol tank was simply painted and then fitted with separate chrome-plated side panels. These panels sat on plastic mats and were held in place by the badges and kneegrips.

The two Featherbed twins were joined by a third twin for 1957, this being the Model 77. While it kept the stock 596 cc 99 engine and gearbox, these were installed in a pivoted-fork frame based on that used by the Model 7. This was because the 77 was intended for sidecar drivers, and it was thought that the extra

The 650SS super sports, or sports special, model introduced for 1962 had twin carburettors mounted on downdraught inlet tracts.

strain of the sidecar could only be catered for by the older type of frame construction.

The Model 77 used normal Roadholder forks and the standard hubs, but the front tyre was of 3.25 in. section. The oil tank and battery box were styled to fit into the subframe corners on each side, and the headlamp shell was of the 1956 pattern with separate panel. The 1957 silencers were fitted, but not the Featherbed dualseat, for the 77 had a flat seat that looked like a plank. The finish was as for the other twins, or in black and grey, but the petrol tank was smaller and only held 3 gallons of fuel.

During 1962 the 745 cc Atlas was introduced, but for export only, hence the high bars.

A 1963 650SS up on a workbench at Norton with retiring sales manager Reg Weeks talking to pressman Peter Howdle.

Both the 88 and 99 had a change to alternator electrics and coil ignition for 1958, a points housing and distributor being fitted in place of the magneto. As the distributor had an auto-advance, it was driven by a plain sprocket, and the system was turned on by a switch combined with the lighting one. The alternator was a Lucas RM15 which went inside the primary chaincase. This was amended to accommodate it and the alternator was spigoted to the crankcase. With the removal of the dynamo, a cover was fitted over the front engine plates.

During the early part of 1958, the option list was extended to include twin carburettors and 9.0:1 pistons for increased power, which came in handy for production racing. Later in the same year came special front forks for sidecar use with reduced trail, heavy-duty springs and a steering damper, all this following the great performance by Eric Oliver in that year's sidecar TT with a fairly stock 88. With the Featherbed frame now well proven for sidecar use, there was no further need for the Model 77, which was dropped at the end of 1958, having had no changes for that year.

For the final year of the decade, 1959, the two twins were treated to a new camshaft and a further option in the shape of a full rear chaincase. The finish remained in the grey, but with alternatives in Post Office red, metalescent blue or black and silver, while chrome-plated mudguards

The Atlas for 1964 in home-market guise with the usual and much preferred Norton flat handlebars.

were a further option.

The changes for 1960 were much more extensive, for they brought a move to the slimline frame and extra models with rear enclosure. The new machines were listed as the 88 de luxe and 99 de luxe, the originals dropping the 'de luxe' tag they had carried since 1956 to become the standard versions.

The rear enclosure was based on that which had been introduced a year earlier for the 249 cc Jubilee twin, and the slimline frame was essential to suit it. The enclosure ran from the cylinder head to the rear number plate and down from the dualseat, but with cut-outs to leave most of the rear wheel in view. There were two side panels, held by Dzus fasteners, and a tail section that was bolted to the machine. The rear number plate could be detached for rear wheel removal, and a lifting handle was provided on the left-hand side.

The de luxe models had deeply valanced front mudguards, while all models had a new dualseat, new silencers (still minus tailpipes), and a revised petrol tank with long, slim badges that included small kneegrips at their ends. The badges acted as dividers for the two-tone paint finish used for all models. The colours could be red, blue or forest green with dove grey for the de luxe models, or red, black or grey with dove grey for the standard ones.

In addition to the frame changes, there were increases in compression ratios to 8.1:1 for the 88 and 7.6:1 for the 99, in both standard and de luxe forms. Only the standard models could have the twin-carburettor option, as the enclosure precluded its use on the de luxe whose frames differed in having the extra brackets needed for its fitment.

There was yet another rise in compression ratios for 1961, the 88 going up to 8.5:1 and the 99 to 8.25:1. The dualseat rear fastening became a Dzus type, and the finishes became specific for each model. Thus, it was green for the standard 88, grey for the 99, red for the de luxe 88 and blue for the similar 99, all of which were combined with dove grey as before.

The range was expanded further early

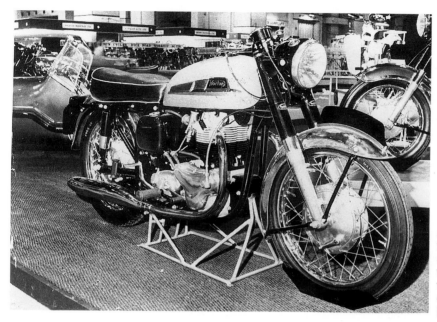

A 1965 650SS from the period when sports machines were all the rage, while tourers and enclosure had fallen by the wayside.

in 1961 with the appearance of a model with an even larger 646 cc capacity engine aimed at the American market. It was listed as the Manxman, and the capacity came from 68 x 89 mm dimenons. The engine, which was fed by twin carburettors on downdraught inlet tracts, had an 8.3:1 compression ratio, a rev-counter drive attached to the timing cover and driven from the camshaft, magneto ignition and a siamesed exhaust.

For cycle parts, in the main, the Manxman used standard Featherbed details, but with high handlebars, a 3.25 in. front tyre section and a 4.00 x 18 in. rear tyre. Its finish was in polychromatic blue

Close-up of a 1967 650SS with its twin carburettors and the downdraught tracts that could make cold starting tricky.

Final year for the Atlas was 1968, by which time it had grown a seat hump and had twin instruments above the headlamp.

and grey, but brightened by chrome-plating for the mudguards and chaincase. When it reached Europe and its home market, much of this had gone and it was listed simply as the '650'. As such, it used the standard twin parts, including tyres, and was finished in two-tone grey.

It was a year for new models in 1961 for, in April, the range was joined by the 88SS and 99SS. Both were sports specials with tuned engines which had better internals, twin carburettors and siamesed exhaust systems. To suit production racing, there were ball-ended control levers and a folding kickstart as standard, and options of a rev-counter and rearsets. The finishes were as for the standard models: green for the 88, grey for the 99, and dove grey as the second colour for both.

The 650 did not reach its home market until late in 1961 when it was joined by de luxe and SS versions. These followed the lines of the smaller models, all three 650s having a new cylinder head with downdraught inlet ports. Only the 650SS had twin carburettors, the others managing with one, and all three had their compression ratio lifted to 8.9:1.

The new cylinder head went on to the 88SS whose compression ratio rose to 9.5:1, while its ignition was changed to magneto with manual advance. The downdraught ports could make cold starting tricky and the engine prone to flooding, but that head was not fitted to the 99SS, which kept the old type with splayed inlet ports. It also retained its coil ignition. The nine-model range had much in common for all three capacities and versions, all changing to an RM19 alternator, but only the SS models to Avon GP rear tyres. The colours remained as for 1961, with the standard and de luxe 650s as the 99 in grey and blue combined with dove grey respectively, and the 650SS in black with a silver tank and the option of chrome-plated mudguards.

Early in 1962 a tenth model joined the range, this being the 745 cc, export-only, Atlas. The capacity came from stretching the engine still further to dimensions of 73 x 89 mm, but the compression ratio was lower at 7.6:1 and only a single carburettor was fitted. This gave the machine its performance in an easier style, so it should have made for a better ride. In practice, the extra capacity made the

The 650SS became the Mercury for 1969 when it changed to a single carburettor and a blue finish for some parts.

vibration level worse. In time, it led to the Commando range covered in the next chapter.

The Atlas engine had magneto ignition, and its engine breather had an elbow fitted to the crankcase in line with the left-hand end of the camshaft. This, along with the engine number prefix, made it easier to spot. On the cycle side, the Atlas was much as the others but, being built mainly for the USA, had a small petrol tank and raised bars. Its finish was as for the 650SS, but with chrome-plated mudguards as standard.

A much smaller range was offered for 1963, as all three 99 models and the de luxe 88 and de luxe 650 were dropped. Enclosure was no longer important but, as always, high performance was. The range that remained comprised standard and SS versions of the 88 and 650 plus the Atlas, all of which ran on with colour changes only.

Very early in 1963, Norton production was transferred to Plumstead, and soon after this the first of a number of hybrids made its appearance, as detailed in a later chapter. Hence the reduced 1963 range, which was further thinned down for 1964 with the removal of the 88 and 650. This only left the two SS models and the Atlas, all of which had their fork legs spaced out, using new crowns, to allow the fitment of wider tyres. All models changed to 12 volt electrics and had steering locks, while the Atlas received twin carburettors and finally reached its home market early in the year.

Not a stock Feather-bed twin, but this Dunstall Dominator is very desirable and has most of the right extras. Nice one.

The three road models continued for 1965 with a wider rear chain in place of the long-standing traditional narrow section used by Norton for so many years. It was much the same for 1966, except for minor colour alterations, but, at the end of that year, the 88SS was dropped.

During 1966, AMC themselves failed. From the resulting financial convulsions was to come Norton-Villiers and the Commando range but, for the rest of the decade, the old Featherbed was to run alongside the new design until phased out.

Naturally, there were few real changes with only the 650SS and Atlas left. For 1967 the changes amounted to the fitting of an RM21 alternator and twin 930 Concentric carburettors in place of the older Monoblocs. Both models had a matching speedometer and rev-counter fitted to a plate held by the fork top-nuts, and the light switch was located between the instruments.

There was a move to a capacitor ignition system and a dualseat with a hump for 1968, but at the end of that year the Atlas was dropped, for its place had been taken by the new Commando model. The 650SS continued alone, but renamed as the Mercury and fitted with only one carburettor. For this model, some details were finished in Atlantic blue, but the tank continued in silver and the frame and forks in black as of old.

With no rev-counter fitted, the earlier twin-instrument mounting plate was amended to carry the speedometer and light switch side by side. They looked rather odd. The model ran on into 1970 in this form with the rev-counter as an option, but during the year the Featherbed twin came to its end.

Prospects

These will always be good for any Featherbed twin, as this was a favoured and popular machine in any model form. For many riders it was preferred to other makes for its frame, while the basic engine was strong and well able to cope with some tuning.

Therefore, they must all rate four stars, even if some are plus and others minus. The basic models, the 88, 99 and 650, have their adherents for being easier to keep in tune, thanks to the single carburettor. The de luxe twins are now quite rare, as they were never as popular as the standard versions, and most lost their panels at some time along the way. Relatively few survive in original condition, which makes them rare, even if not the most sought after.

The reverse applies to the SS models, as there are more about, but there are also more people seeking them and they rate a plus. To get this, originality is essential, so beware of a machine which has been converted from standard to sports. The performance of all is good, even that of the smallest engine. Some riders have found the 88 the most pleasant to ride on the road, both at speed and in traffic.

The Atlas offers the greatest capacity, but also the most vibration, so it may not be the choice of the regular rider. A smaller twin, or one of the Commando models, could be more suitable. However, for sheer low-down power and easy cruising, it has much to offer. Finally, there is the Mercury, which offers the simple tune of a single carburettor matched to the SS-type engine. Maybe minus four stars because it is younger than the others and not from the real Featherbed period.

The Model 77 is another rare one, but really only commands three stars, for it is not as desirable as the Featherbed models. It failed to fit in or strike much of a note in its day and is unlikely to raise many ripples now. Nice as a big four-stroke twin, but the others are to be preferred.

Regardless of model or year, the twin offers fine motorcycling from a type that has set the standard for handling since it was introduced. For owners, the finish, whether in the usual polychromatic grey, bright Post Office red or traditional Norton black and silver, has always been dignified and stylish, setting a seal of approval on their choice.

★★★	497 cc	88 Nomad	1960
★★★	596 cc	99 Nomad	1958-60
★★★	745 cc	Atlas MX	1963-64
★★★	745 cc	N15CS 'N'	1964-67
★★★	745 cc	N15CS	1968
★★★	745 cc	P11	1967
★★★	745 cc	P11A	1968
★★★	745 cc	Ranger	1968
★★★	745 cc	G15	1965-67
★★★	745 cc	G15MkII	1968-69
★★★★	745 cc	G15CSR	1965-69
★★★	745 cc	G15CS	1967-69
★★★	745 cc	33	1965-67
★★★★	745 cc	33CSR	1965-67

Off-road and hybrid twins

Norton were a firm that was generally associated with road racing, rather than off-road events, although they had their successes in both trials and scrambles. Their off-road singles appeared in the early post-war period and have already been covered, while the twins belonged to a later era. As such, they were aimed more at the enduro or trail event than scrambles where their weight told against them.

The big Atlas engine was used for most of these off-road models and also served a series of hybrids built in the second half of the 1960s. These appeared under the AJS and Matchless labels, but used as many parts of Norton origin as of AMC. They represent a confusing period in Norton history, but one that a prospective owner and buyer needs to know about, if only to avoid.

The export-only 99 Nomad of 1958 with its tuned 99 engine, model 77 frame, 21 in. front wheel and off-road fitments.

Off-road twins

The first signs of these appeared in 1958 when the export-only 99 Nomad made its appearance for the American enduro market. The model was essentially a scrambler with lights, using the Model 77 frame which was more suited to off-road use than the Featherbed with its wide bottom rails. The 77 frame was narrower where it counted on the trail and came with an undershield as well.

The power unit was a tuned version of the 99 engine with a 9.0:1 compression ratio, twin carburettors and a siamesed exhaust system. Ignition continued to be by magneto, but the lights were powered by a Lucas alternator. The transmission and hubs were stock, as were the Roadholder forks, but the front tyre size went out to a 21 in. diameter and the rear tyre was of a fatter section, both having a trail pattern.

Light-alloy mudguards and a small tank set the machine off, and the finish was bright thanks to a white seat top and red tank with chrome-plated side panels. Both the mudguards and the lower fork legs were polished. Seat, oil tank and left-hand side cover all came from the Model 77, and the headlamp had the light switch set in it. Stands were provided, but could be removed for an event.

For 1963 Norton brought out this Atlas MX, which was more of a trail or enduro machine than a scrambler.

The Nomad continued in this form for two further years and was joined by a 497 cc version for 1960 only. The 88 Nomad, as it was known, copied the larger model in all respects, except in having coil ignition. Both models were dropped at the end of that season.

After that, there were no off-road twins for some three years, but in August 1963 the firm introduced the Atlas MX, a scrambles model using a combination of Norton and AMC parts. This was another result of the amalgamation of the two companies and the move of Norton production to Plumstead. The outcome was that the Atlas MX had the twin-carburettor Atlas engine and common AMC gearbox installed in a frame from an AMC sports twin model. To this were added Norton forks, wheels and brakes, while the seat, silencers and petrol tank were all of AMC origin.

Although the machine was intended as a scrambler, it came with full road equipment, lights, a speedometer and rev-counter. In truth, it was much more a trail model. Even for enduro use, it would have been essential to change the low-mounted silencers and close-fitting front mudguard, but at least an undershield was provided.

During 1964 the model's name was changed to N15CS'N', but there was little real alteration otherwise. For 1968, it was altered again to the N15CS, by which time it had gained gaitered forks, a new seat and more sporting front mudguard, but little more. At the end of that year the model was dropped.

A second off-road twin had been introduced for 1967 as the P11. At first sight, this differed little from the N15CS, for it used the twin-carburettor Atlas engine, now fitted with Concentrics, an alternator, a cast-alloy chaincase and an AMC gearbox. However, the mechanics were assembled into a Matchless G85CS scrambles model frame fitted with AMC

For 1964 the Atlas MX became the N15CS'N' and, for 1968 the N15CS shown here.

gaitered forks, and it rode on AMC hubs with 7 in. brakes. The tyre sizes were 3.25 x 19 in. front and 4.00 x 18 in. rear, both being of a trail pattern, while each exhaust pipe was tucked up to run back at waist level to a small tubular silencer.

The oil tank was fitted into the subframe on the right-hand side of the machine and was matched by a cover on the left. Full lights and instruments were fitted, along with a short single seat and a prop stand. The finish was in Candy Apple red for the petrol tank with polished light-alloy mudguards, the result being a machine with style that caught the public's eye, especially in the USA.

For 1968 the model became the P11A with a change to the exhaust systems, which now swept down and ran back at low level to tilted silencers with small reverse-cone ends. Late in the year the name was changed yet again to the Ranger, but this made little difference, for the model was dropped at the end of

Final version of the off-road twin was this Ranger model built for a few months late in 1968.

The standard AJS version of the hybrid twins was the model 33, this being a 1966 model.

The Matchless standard equivalent was the G15, and this one is from 1965, hence the massive tank badges.

the year. Like many, it was a victim of the trauma the whole group was then suffering.

Prospects

Three even stars for all the off-road twins with maybe a plus for a Nomad as a rare model and one for the P11 for style. These were never mainstream machines, but they had their adherents and followers.

Of these models, the P11 and P11A are perhaps the most sought after. They were lighter, therefore easier to handle on the trail, while holding a stylish line for boulevard cruising. The Ranger is a rare one, as it was produced for such a short time, while the Atlas scrambler, in its various guises, seemed to lack the style of the P11. These machines will not handle as well as the Featherbed on the road, but this was not their forte. Their

world was the trail and the desert where they worked well.

Hybrid twins

In the mid-1960s the AMC group was in serious financial trouble and ready to grasp any passing straw. One such was to enlarge their existing twin engine to suit the American market, the result was the export-only G15/45 with 750 cc AMC motor. This stretched version of their vibration-prone 650 engine was never sold on the home market, and it was not too successful in the USA. Consequently, the firm turned to the Norton Atlas as a readily available group product, even if it was equally prone to vibration.

The result was the AJS 33 and 33CSR, plus the Matchless G15 and G15CSR models which appeared for 1965. These had the stock Atlas engine installed in the AMC frame, but fitted with Norton Roadholder forks and Norton hubs and brakes. The gearbox remained the common AMC type, and a cast light-alloy chaincase concealed the primary transmission.

The CSR models had a real line to them in the café racer mould - rearsets, lovely swept-back exhaust pipes, low bars and reversed gear pedal. Their finish was bright and sporting, as were their mudguards and dualseat. The standard models were more conventional, having stock bars, exhaust, footrests and seat.

These hybrids ran on in AJS form to 1967, after which the 33 and 33CSR were no longer offered. The more popular Matchless pair continued, having been joined for 1967 by the street scrambler G15CS, which was built for export. This had twin 930 carburettors, which went on the other models that year, and trail tyres. For 1968 the G15 became the G15MkII with capacitor ignition, also used by the other models. All trickled on into 1969 when the factory closed.

Prospects

The hybrid twins are not Nortons, even though the engine, gearbox, forks, hubs and brakes are. On a star scale, they rate three for the basic machines and four for the CSR models, for these are collectable motorcycles with their own enthusiasts and club. While not Nortons, the buyer needs to know about them and how they fit into the Norton and AMC pattern. Be careful if offered one as a Norton or as suitable for spares. Much was common, but not all, so beware. For instance, the gearbox shell varies, and so may its mainshaft. Could be painful and costly if these points are not spotted.

Sports versions of both hybrids were built. This is the 1965 Matchless G15CSR with lovely exhaust pipe line.

84

Chapter 7

Commando twins

★★★★	745 cc 20M3	1968-69
★★★★	745 cc R	1969
★★★★	745 cc S	1969-70
★★★★	745 cc Fastback	1969-73
★★★★	745 cc Fastback LR	1971-73
★★★★	745 cc Roadster	1970-73
★★★★	745 cc Street Scrambler	1971
★★★★★	745 cc Production Racer	1971-73
★★★	745 cc Hi-Rider	1971-73
★★★★	745 cc Interstate	1972-73
★★★★	829 cc Roadster	1973-77
★★★★	829 cc Interstate	1973-77
★★★	829 cc Hi-Rider	1973-75
★★★★★	829 cc John Player Norton	1973-75
★★★★★	749 cc Thruxton Club racer	1975

Once Norton-Villiers was established, the firm soon decided that they needed a new big twin to replace the Atlas. Their first thought was to revive an experimental overhead-camshaft model known as the P10, but its inherent problems decided against it and new parameters were laid down. These included no, or minimal, vibration (as this was a sore point with the Atlas), new styling to retain some degree of the Norton line in a more modern and aggressive form, and a new name - Commando.

The Commando broke new ground with its Isolastic system which insulated the rider from engine vibration. This was done by assembling the engine, gearbox,

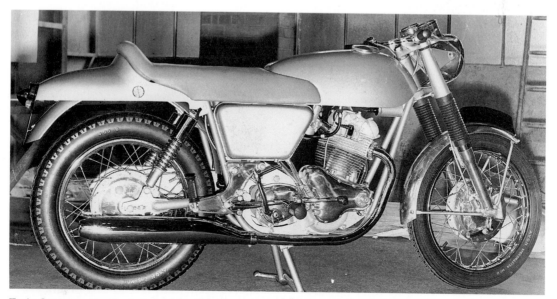

Early Commando prior to launch in 1967, hence lack of tank badges, showing the lines of tank, seat and tail unit.

Close-up of 1967 primary chaincase, footrest support, rest and rear brake mounting.

pivoted rear fork and back wheel as one unit and attaching this to the frame with rubber mountings. These were designed to allow movement in the planes along the machine's axis, but to prevent tilt. In all respects, the system was successful, although the engine vibration was still there.

Early Commando 1968-71

The Commando was first seen at Earls Court in September 1967 and went into production early in 1968. While the frame and many of its fittings were new, there was a good deal from the past among the mechanics, the engine, gearbox, forks, hubs and brakes all being familiar to Norton owners.

The engine was the 745 cc Atlas with a 9.0:1 compression ratio and twin 930 Concentric carburettors. It was inclined forward a little to give a different line to

the machine, and this forced the use of curved inlet tracts to keep the carburettors at a reasonable angle and clear of the underside of the petrol tank. Ignition was by twin coils and a capacitor, powered by the Lucas RM21 alternator.

The gearbox was the standard AMC type with a revised shell and other minor changes. A triplex primary chain was used and, for the launch model, a conventional six-plate clutch. In production, the clutch was changed to one with a diaphragm spring to clamp the plates. This lacked the shock absorber of the conventional type. A massive light-alloy chaincase enclosed the clutch and primary drive. It had screwed plugs to allow the ignition timing to be checked with a strobe light, the clutch to be adjusted, the chain tension to be checked, and oil to be added.

Engine, gearbox and chaincase formed

The tail unit offered limited storage for the tool roll, with access by seat removal.

a single assembly along with front and rear mountings, the last also supporting the rear fork. The mountings had the Isolastic fittings installed in them, and these were supplemented by a top steady which was bolted to the rocker box. The front mounting was simply a large cross-tube to which were welded two engine plates that were bolted to the front of the crankcase. The rear mounting was similar, but its plates extended back and around the gearbox with the cross-tube welded in at the top rear corner. Beneath it went a second tube which carried a pivot pin on whose ends the rear fork oscillated.

The frame itself looked conventional with a single, large-diameter, top tube, twin downtubes which ran under the engine and gearbox before turning up to

the rear unit top mountings, and bracing tubes running across the subframe corners. The headstock was braced to the top tube by a gusset at first, but this proved inadequate, so an extra tube was added beneath the top one to add stiffness.

Assembly of the engine unit and the frame was with the Isolastic mountings at front and rear. In essence, each mounting cross-tube was centred on a spindle bolted to frame lugs with two sets of rubbers between tube and spindle to maintain their positions. Side movement was closely controlled and adjusted to specific fine limits. In the original design, this was done using a vernier system of adjustment, but this was ruled out for production, on the grounds of costs, so shims were used instead. These needed regular servicing and adjustment which, if neglected, could upset the handling.

The engine-to-frame mounting was completed by the head steady which kept the whole thing upright and in line. Unfortunately, the early design was prone to fracture and was eventually modified, but not until 1973. Most have now been changed, and any that have not, should be.

The shims can be arranged to control the gap between the mountings and frame, and production racers often had a smaller gap which gave more precise handling, even if the vibration began to be noticed again. Some gap remained essential, however, as without it the parts became solid and the frame broke.

As the silencers were held rigidly to the engine by the exhaust pipes, their mountings to the frame had to be flexible. These were made with further rubbers which were attached to a forged light-alloy support plate on each side of the machine. These plates were placed just to the rear of the chaincase and the gearbox. They carried the footrests and pillion rests as well as the silencer mountings.

Front suspension was by short Roadholder forks, much as used by the other twins, but with a small change of stanchion length. The front hub was the usual full-width, light-alloy component, but it was fitted with the 8 in. twin-leading-shoe brake previously offered as a Featherbed twin option. The hub was

A batch of model 20M3 Commandos at the factory in May 1968. Later the model was named the Fastback.

spoked into a steel rim fitted with a 3.00 x 19 in. tyre. At the rear went the standard, and similar, hub with 7 in. brake. That wheel had a 3.50 x 19 in. tyre.

For the rest, there were sports mudguards, the rear one being nearly out of sight under a glass-fibre tail unit which ran from the rear light forward under the dualseat. The petrol tank was in glass-fibre and had a snap-action cap, while the oil tank went on the right-hand side of the machine and was matched by a panel on the left. Between tank and panel went the 12 volt battery and other electrics, the ignition switch being just ahead of the panel on a frame bracket.

The dualseat was orange at the show, but black in production, and had an ear on each side which ran forward to form a kneegrip. The tank decor included a round tank badge plus a smaller round green disc on each side. The green spot represented world markets, but confused

potential buyers. The spots were repeated on the tail unit and the dials of the speedometer and rev-counter, which sat side by side on the fork crown.

An air filter assembly went between the oil tank and side panel with connections to both carburettors, while the silencers were the stock type without tail pipes, as used by other models. The show finish was mainly silver and chrome-plating, but for production it was black frame and cylinder block, green petrol tank and tail unit, silver oil tank and side panel, black seat, and chrome-plated mudguards and wheel rims. The chaincase and lower fork legs were polished.

The Commando was an immediate success with press and public, and it went on sale as the 20M3 model. Both custom and performance kits were shown in brochures at the launch, but none seemed to reach production. This had no real effect

Neale Shilton with an early Interpol and the Lady Mayor of Andover in 1970.

The high-level, left-side exhaust system was one of the main styling features of the model S built for 1969-70.

on its impact on customers and riders, for such was the machine's success that it won the prestigious *Motor Cycle News* 'Machine of the Year' poll for 1968. It was to continue to take this title for another four years right up to 1972.

After its launch, the Commando was altered little in its basic format. There were many model variations, brought about by mainly cosmetic changes to the tank, mudguards and side panels, while there were mechanical changes in time to the engine, brakes and finish. However, the essential Commando frame, forks, engine and gearbox remained in the pattern set by the first prototype.

The block finish became silver for 1969, and in March that year the original machine became the Fastback and was joined by the R and the S models. Neither had the tail unit of the Fastback, being fitted with a stock rear mudguard instead. The R was aimed at the American street scrambler market, for which it had a small

blue or red petrol tank, a normal dualseat and high bars. The S was similar in most respects.

The most obvious change for the S was to the exhaust system, for both pipes curled round to the left to run, one above the other, at waist level along the top of the chaincase. The silencers were of reverse-cone form and continued the line, while both sections of the system were fitted with a perforated heat shield to protect the rider. The S was fitted with slimline forks without gaiters, a protector ring around the headlamp and a side panel on each side, these being smaller than those used by the other models.

The engine fitted to the S models differed from the original design in having the ignition points mounted in the timing cover, with their cam and its auto-advance driven from the end of the camshaft. Thus, the hard-to-service distributor and its chain drive went, but a new means was needed to drive the rev-counter. This was achieved by cutting a skew gear on the camshaft and fitting a cable housing in the top of the crankcase for the driven shaft which meshed with it. Some R machines had the engine with the timing-cover points, but that model was only built for part of 1969.

During 1969, production moved again, engine and gearbox manufacture going to the Villiers plant in Wolverhampton, while assembly took place at Andover in Hampshire. The 120-mile gap and split responsibility was to create many problems over the years to come. The one asset was the proximity of Thruxton race circuit where the test department and, later, a performance shop were set up.

The Fastback went over to the timing cover points in September 1969 and, together with the S, was joined by the Roadster in March 1970. This was essentially an S with low-level exhaust systems. All three models were offered with several choices of colour for the petrol tank and side covers, plus the tail unit for the Fastback.

During 1970, the S was dropped, and in September the Fastback was fitted with the reverse-cone silencers of the Roadster to become the Mk II. This was very short-lived, for January 1971 brought in the Fastback Mk III and Roadster Mk II. Both had the slimline forks without gaiters,

while the handlebars had Lucas controls with the switches built into the pivot blocks. Other changes were to sealed ball races for the headstock bearings, which worked very well, a shock absorber in the rear hub, and a new oil tank plus right-hand side cover for the Fastback.

During 1971 four further models joined the two already available, but all kept to the basic Commando concept. First to appear was the Street Scrambler, which had a waist-level exhaust pipe and reverse-cone silencer on each side. To suit its intended use, it had an undershield, braced handlebars, and small headlamp and petrol tank, while a sprung front mudguard was fitted. A bright yellow or tangerine colour was used for the tank, but the model was only listed for a few months.

The next two models arrived together, one being the Fastback LR and the other the Production Racer. The former was a stock Fastback fitted with a larger petrol tank to justify the 'Long Range' tag and, due to the tank, a dualseat to suit. The Production Racer was rather more serious and stemmed from a prototype built in 1969 and others built in 1970 at the Norvil performance shop.

For this model, the engine was tuned and the machine fitted with rearsets, a cockpit fairing and clip-ons. A long list of

The Roadster model was much as the S, but with low-level exhausts. This is a 1970 machine, the model's first year.

With his thoughts far away on the race track, one rider tries a 1970 Production Racer for size.

options included a disc front brake, close-ratio gears with four or five speeds, and many detail parts for racing. It added up to a very quick machine which had many successes in both production and 750 cc racing. The 1971 Production Racer was fitted with a Lockheed disc front brake as standard and finished in yellow.

The last of the new 1971 models was the Hi-Rider, which came in a chopper, or custom, style. To suit this, it had the small tank and side panels, very high-rise unbraced handlebars, and an odd dualseat with extreme rear hump. It hardly fitted in with the Norton image, but nearly all of it was stock Commando, so it was easy enough to produce.

During this period, one further version of the Commando appeared on the road, although it was not for the public. This was the Interpol, which was produced for police forces using mainly standard parts. Alterations comprised a choice of steel tanks, with or without a radio recess, a single seat, a special speedometer, panniers for equipment, a fairing with blue lamp and, usually, a white finish with suitable police and safety stripes.

The Interpol was first built in 1970 and was to continue in production alongside the standard models until 1976. During this period, it received the general changes which went into all the machines, some good and some bad, and was, overall, successful in its job.

The standard model Fastback, LR, Roadster, Production Racer, and Hi-Rider all ran on for 1972, but with engine modifications that were to have far-reaching effects.

Prospects

All Commandos have their weak points and faults, but these can be overcome to produce a fine, fast motorcycle. Any owner, or prospective owner, is strongly recommended to obtain a copy

The rather strange Hi-Rider, which was introduced for 1971 with very raised bars and special seat.

of 'Commando Service Notes', a booklet produced by the British Norton Owners Club. This goes through the machine, section by section, and covers, in great detail, what can go wrong and how to deal with it.

Typical of the problems are those centred on the rear fork pivot and its lubrication. This was intended to be by oil, but owners often used grease and the result was worn-out parts. Similar troubles can be found all over the machine, but there are solutions.

Because the machines have the potential to be used on a daily basis in today's traffic, while retaining their classic features, they generally qualify for four stars. Only the Hi-Rider drops to three, due to its odd nature, while the Production Racer has to rate five stars.

Some models, such as the R, Street Scrambler and Fastback LR, are much rarer than the others, so they may qualify for a plus with their stars. The same could apply to any early model 20M3, but less so for stock Fastback and Roadster machines. The S is more common in its own country than some others and gets a plus for its sheer style!

The Combat fiasco 1972-73

The four road machines became Mk IV models for 1972 when they were joined by one new machine, the Interstate, which was built for touring. For this, it was fitted with a petrol tank able to carry over five gallons of fuel, while its silencers were of a new form with short, shallow-taper megaphone and long reverse-cone.

All models had a revised crankcase which introduced internal webs to increase the support for the main bearings, while the timing-side main became a roller race to match the drive-side bearing. In this way, the crankshaft location was lost and it floated between the roller races with shims to limit the end-play, never a good arrangement.

Other changes were to remove the sump filter, so the scavenge pump was no longer protected from debris, and to add a cartridge oil filter to the return line, this being mounted between the engine and gearbox. The timed engine breather

The Interstate was introduced for 1972, and most were fitted with the trouble-some Combat engine and disc front brake.

was no longer used and in its place went a separator bolted to the back of the crankcase, low down, with a pipe running from it to the oil tank.

A high-performance version of the engine became available as an option for the Roadster and Interstate, being called the Combat. Its power came from an increase in compression ratio (achieved by skimming the cylinder head), larger 932 carburettors and a revised camshaft. Such engines had the block painted black. A further option for the same models was a disc front brake, based on the racing one, but with the caliper on the right, behind the fork leg. A final change was to 4.10 in. section tyres for both wheels.

The changes combined with other factors to give owners major problems. The engine design had been stretched to 50 per cent more capacity, higher rpm and twice the power of the original, so it began to object. The crankshaft would flex, which conflicted with the new, stiffer crankcase and its roller bearings on each side, resulting in the roller corners digging into the race tracks.

Other factors which amplified the effects were varied. One was the low gearing which allowed any owner to pull 7000 rpm in top gear - which they did. Inside the engine were Atlas slotted pistons, which were fine for 5000 rpm, but prone to the crown pulling off the skirt at the 7000 rpm Combat engines were running to. Allied to this was a camshaft drive whose chain was seldom correctly adjusted, as it was an awkward job to do correctly. This would vary the ignition timing, which was made worse by an inadequate auto-advance mechanism that could fluctuate or simply jam in one position.

All this combined to reduce main bearing life to an unacceptably low level - even when the pistons stayed in one piece. There was no single answer to the problem, but the mains themselves were changed to a Superblend design where each roller in the race had a slight barrel form at its ends and, thus, could cope with both the speed and the flexing. The

A 1972 Fastback which continued with the original Commando style, but only for one more year.

pistons were no longer slotted so stayed in one piece, and the ignition advance was much improved. The gearing was raised so that owners could no longer reach peak rpm in top gear, and this gave the machine a more restful manner.

This work took time, and Norton realised that the improvements were essential, so they decided to drop the Combat specification and rework all the engines. This meant that every complete machine had to go down the assembly line to be dismantled, after which its engine was returned to Wolverhampton for rework, and then the whole process was reversed for assembly. The one area that proved really awkward to correct was the compression ratio, and various solutions using thick or twin gaskets were never totally successful.

It made 1972 a bad year, but in the end the machines were much improved and many of the changes went into older models as time went by. Thus, the Superblend mains are now the normal replacement for any Commando, along with many other detail modifications.

The 1973 range was announced in March, but this did not include the two Fastback models. The Roadster, Interstate and Hi-Rider continued in a Mk V form with the option of turn signals, which had only been listed for the Interstate for 1972. The engines kept the 932 carburettors, as used by the Combat, which worked well with the reduced compression ratio and raised gearing. Only the Hi-Rider had the 8 in. front brake, the other two models having the disc at the front. The Production Racer continued in the lists and was joined by a Formula 750 Racer, which was fitted with a fairing and retained the yellow finish.

After the trauma of 1972, the firm suf-

Roadster of 1972 outside the Norton Villiers works and still fitted with the drum front brake.

fered from external events in 1973 as they became involved in the happenings at BSA and Triumph, from which came Norton Villiers Triumph, or NVT. In the autumn came the start of the Triumph workers' sit-in at Meriden, and Norton became just one more pawn among many being manipulated at high level.

Despite this, a large replacement Commando had been introduced in April 1973 to take over from the 745 cc models which came to their end late in the year.

Prospects

Machines built during the Combat engine trauma still rate their four stars, with five for the Production Racer and three for the Hi-Rider. By now, all the Combat engines, and many others, will have received Superblend mains, the improved auto-advance and some arrangement to reduce the compression ratio.

This work makes the 1973 745 cc engines the best of the bunch but, as any engine can be brought up to scratch, this is more of an academic point now. Should a machine surface with its original Combat specification, then it will need working on and the price adjusted accord-

The 1973 Hi-Rider which changed little during its lifetime, but was also built with the 829 cc engine and disc front brake.

ingly.

That aspect aside, the choice between Fastback, Roadster, LR, Interstate and Hi-Rider is dictated by riding style and the owner's needs. The two versions of the Fastback were only built with the 745 cc engine, but the other three went on to bigger and better cubes!

The 829 cc Commando 1973-74

The firm had one final stretch for Bert Hopwood's 1948 design, which took the bore out to 77 mm and the capacity to 829 cc, while leaving most other aspects of the specification as they were. The engine was fitted to Roadster, Interstate and Hi-Rider models which all carried an '850' label, even if the actual capacity was lower.

To achieve the larger bore, there was a new block which had the casting extended out to each side. This allowed the use of long fixing bolts which ran down through the block into the top of the crankcase. On the inside there was an adjustment to the flywheel weight to suit the new pistons, and on the underside, the sump filter returned. The breathing system was much improved by venting the crankcase to the timing chest and fitting an outlet pipe in the upper rear corner where the magneto had once lived.

Externally, there was a balance pipe between the exhausts, close up to the port, and reverse-cone silencers for the Roadster and Hi-Rider, but the short megaphone with long reverse-cone remained on the Interstate. All models had the disc front brake, and only the Hi-Rider a glass-fibre petrol tank.

In September 1973 Mk IA versions of the Roadster and Interstate appeared for

A 1973 829 cc Roadster with a balance pipe between the exhausts and familiar Commando fitments.

the European market and joined the original Mk I models, which continued for a little while. The Mk IA machines had a reduced noise level which was achieved using new silencers and an enlarged air filter box. The silencers had a megaphone taper and long body which ended with matt black end mutes. They soon became known as the 'bean can' or 'black cap' silencers, and they worked well, reduced the noise, did not affect the power and became the recommended fit for all.

Around this time a special short-stroke engine was offered, either as a unit or fitted to a Roadster model. The stroke was reduced to 80.4 mm, which combined with the 77 mm bore to give a 749

cc capacity. The engine had high-compression pistons, a hot camshaft, big valves, steel rods and electronic ignition, all to improve the performance. It was suggested that the Roadster with this engine could be used for fast road work or as the basis of a road racing machine. To this end, there were further options of 33 mm carburettors and megaphone exhaust systems.

At this time the company was actively racing Commando-based machines with sponsorship from the John Player tobacco company. This led to the introduction of the John Player Norton, or JPN, late in 1973, with production reaching the public in the following April.

The JPN used the standard Commando

The Roadster MkIA of 1974 with large black airbox and 'bean can' silencers.

mechanics with the 749 cc short-stroke engine as an option. Alterations amounted to a high-output alternator, to provide power for twin headlamps, and matt black exhaust pipes with 'bean can' silencers to suit the overall style.

What set the JPN apart was its bodywork, for the model came as standard with a fairing, screen, dummy tank and tail unit. The fairing included an instrument panel, had the two headlight units side by side in its nose, and had a turn signal lamp and a mirror on each side. The dummy tank cover concealed a steel petrol tank and was bolted into the fairing to increase its rigidity.

As standard, the JPN was fitted with clip-ons and rearsets, while the tail unit carried the padding for the single seat. The finish was mainly white, this being the base colour for the fairing and other glass-fibre mouldings, which included a brief front mudguard. Relief was provided by stripes on the fairing and tail

unit, as well as by the Norton transfer on the tank cover.

For 1974 the Mk IA Interstate and Roadster models continued, while the Mk I versions became Mk IIA with the new airbox, bean-can silencers and a pleated seat top. Some for the USA kept the earlier intake and exhaust systems for, while the silencers were fine, the air box reduced the performance. The Hi-Rider simply became the Mk II and kept its original filter and silencers.

In this way, the Roadster and Interstate, in Mk IA and IIA forms, plus the Mk II Hi-Rider and JPN, continued to early 1975. By then, the NVT saga was nearing the end of the Meriden sit-in, but other external events had major effects on the group. These included massive inflation and an energy crisis, during which Norton had to struggle on as best it could.

The result was a much reduced 1975 range with some major alterations to the

John Player Norton, or JPN, offered for 1974 and the result of sponsorship the firm received from that tobacco company.

Final 1973 Interstate with its large petrol tank and much improved engine, perhaps the best of the 745 cc units.

A 1974 Production Racer being admired by Prince Albert of Liege at the Brussels show.

specification, although the basic Commando remained in the original form.

Prospects

Four stars for the Roadster and Interstate, three for the Hi-Rider and five for the John Player Norton, so not much changes from the 750 models. Aside from the extra capacity, and minor alterations, there is no real difference between the two sizes, so the choice is down to individual preference and availability of machines.

Some owners prefer the extra size for the easier manner in which it pulls the machine along, but the difference is small. Suffice to say that the 850 missed the Combat and main bearing problems of the 750, benefited from the resultant im-

provements, and is perhaps slightly more desirable that the smaller machine!

The Mk III 850 1975-77

There were three models listed for 1975, the Roadster, Interstate and a few Hi-Riders in MkIII form, while the Interpol continued and was given the same alterations as the others. The changes were quite extensive, for the gearchange and rear brake pedals switched sides, a disc rear brake and notional electric start appeared, and there was vernier adjustment for the Isolastic mountings.

The revisions to the mountings made their setting much easier, and the system could be fitted to earlier machines, so some owners took advantage of this. The

The 1975 MkIII Roadster with electric start of a sort, rear disc brake and left-side gearchange.

rear mounting was a direct swop, but the front required a simple modification.

The main change was the reversal of the pedals, the rear brake pedal position being easier to arrange. It was moved to the right-hand side of the machine, and with this change the rear brake became a disc. The rear hub was modified to take this on the right-hand side, but continued with the sprocket and shock absorber on the left.

The rear brake pedal was pivoted on the footrest hanger and linked to a hydraulic master cylinder mounted on the support plate. This cylinder was connected to a hydraulic caliper. For the front wheel, the caliper was moved to the left side, ahead of the fork leg, as this improved the handling for some obscure technical reason.

Fitting the gear pedal on the left was not so easy, and the adopted solution was to positively locate the gearbox in its mounting and extend the gear pedal shaft across the machine to the left. For this, it had to pass through the primary chaincase where a spur-gear pair enabled the pedal pivot to be set back to a better position. With the gearbox fixed, it was necessary to add tensioners for each run of the primary chain, which was done with a twin-plunger device.

The electric starter was bolted to the back of the inner chaincase, which was new, the two light-alloy halfs being held together by a row of screws, and not the more usual single nut. The starter drove the left-hand end of the crankshaft via a gear train and roller clutch, but was never a great success, offering assistance only at the best of times. Owners were glad that the kickstart had been retained.

Other mechanical changes were the addition of an anti-drain valve in the oil supply line (a long awaited improvement) and an inspection plug in the timing cover, plus the deletion of the over-enthusiastic rear chain oiler. Detail im-

A MkIII Interpol with the 829 cc engine on show at Wolverhampton for a police guest day in 1975.

provements brought in a hinged dualseat, fork gaiters for European machines and a small console between the rev-counter and speedometer for the ignition switch and warning lights. The other switches were grouped in the control lever bodies and much improved from their earlier type.

The two main models differed only in dualseat, side covers and petrol tank, the last two items being the only coloured ones on the machine. This made for ease of production and caused little trouble in changing the colour if the customer wished it. The Interpol had its own tank, seat, valanced mudguards and handlebar, the petrol tank being listed with pommels or a radio recess.

In addition to the normal models, the firm listed the Thruxton Club racing machine, which was hand-built in very small numbers. It used the short-stroke 749 cc engine fitted with its full-race options and drove a five-speed gearbox. The Commando frame was retained along with disc brakes, to which were added alloy rims and a fairing. The Thruxton Club really came too late for, by 1975, the racing world was riding the TZ Yamaha, with the RG Suzuki soon to become available as well. For the club rider, the TZ was much easier to cope with, so the Norton twin disappeared as fast as it had come.

There were further commercial changes around that time but, for the

Official picture of the MkIII Commando Interstate of 1975 and the final form of that model.

Commando, the end was approaching fast. The firm continued with the two models for 1976, and a batch of 1500 machines was built in 1977. A few more were assembled early the next year, and one more surfaced as late as 1982.

For practical purposes, the Commando's run ended in 1977 and with this came the end of the 30-year-old design of the Norton twin engine.

Prospects

Good for any Mk III, with four stars for the Roadster and Interstate on the lines of the earlier machines. Whether you prefer early or late is largely a matter of individual taste, needs and opportunities, the late models being the most developed. The electric start may be viewed as a joke by the Owner's Club, but it can always be ignored, or even removed.

For the Thruxton Club, it has to be five stars because it is rare, not for any other reason. As a machine, it is not as desirable as the Production Racer, but for a really rare model it earns its stars.

The Thruxton Club
Racer of 1975,
which was built in
small numbers and
used the short-
stroke 749 cc
engine in full-race
trim.

Tuner Ray Petty
seated on the last
Norton built in
1982 as a late-
type MkIII Inter-
state.

Not a stock Commando, but one with the extras offered by London dealer Gus Kuhn, and now much sort after.

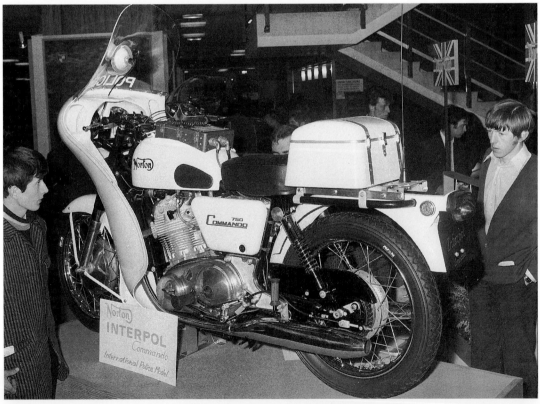

An early 745 cc Commando Interpol, and a model that some enthusiasts would find an attractive alternative.

Chapter 8

Lightweight twins

In 1958, Norton decided to enter the 250 cc market, choosing a machine with a twin-cylinder engine. It was named the Jubilee, to celebrate the 60 years since James Norton had founded his original company, and it was shown to the public at Earls Court late in 1958. The Jubilee broke away from Norton tradition in a good many ways for, as well as the small-capacity, twin-cylinder engine, it featured unit construction, a built-up frame, rear enclosure and a two-colour finish.

The original layout of the engine unit was conceived by Bert Hopwood, but was completely different from the Dominator twin. One feature that was not to reach production was for each head and barrel to be die-cast as one light-alloy piece. This was feasible thanks to the large bore and narrow valve angle, but it never came to pass.

The engine was based on 60 x 44 mm

Jubilee 249 cc twin of 1959, which introduced the Norton rear enclosure also seen on the larger de luxe twins.

Show time for the launch of the Jubilee, which broke Norton tradition by having a name rather than a number.

Timing-side of the 1959 Jubilee, which differed in many ways from the Dominator design.

The larger 349 cc Navigator, which used the Roadholder forks and full-width, light-alloy, front brake from the larger twins.

dimensions, so the capacity came out at 249 cc. The design was conventional in most respects, with a vertical crankcase joint on the centre-line of the engine running back through the gearbox shell, which was cast in unit with the two case halves. Inside went a one-piece nodular-iron crankshaft formed with a slim central flywheel.

The crankshaft was supported by main bearings of the same size as used in the Dominator twin, with a roller on the drive-side and a ball race on the timing-side. Although the Jubilee main bearings were of the same dimensions as those of the larger twins, they differed in having a large radius on the inner bore to match that of the crankshaft. If the wrong bearing type is fitted, it will break the cases.

The light-alloy connecting rods had split big-ends with shell bearings but the gudgeon pins ran directly in the small-ends. The compression ratio was 8.75:1, each three-ring piston having a flat top and moving in its own cast-iron cylinder, which was deeply spigoted into the crankcase.

Each separate cylinder head was cast in light-alloy and incorporated rocker supports and wells for the valves. The inlet ports were parallel with a separate light-alloy manifold which was bolted in place and carried a Type 375 Monobloc carburettor of 25/32 in. bore. The exhaust ports were well splayed out, the pipes being a push-fit into them, and each pipe was fitted with a stock Norton silencer.

The valve gear was controlled by twin camshafts mounted high up in the crankcase to front and rear of the crankshaft. They were gear driven from the right-hand end of the crankshaft which had a small pinion that meshed with an inter-

The chairman of AMC with the Electra 400 in 1963, Norton's first use of an electric starter.

mediate gear which, in turn, drove the camshafts. The tappets above the cams were fitted into guides that were pressed into the cylinders, and these lay at an angle out from the bore line. Very short pushrods then took the cam motion to the rockers, which were fore and aft of the valves and not in the usual cross-over layout.

Each valve moved in a guide, pressed in to a circlip location, and was restrained by duplex coil springs seated on a cup located to the guide. A collar and collets retained the springs, while the valve clearance was set using eccentric rocker spindles. Once set, the spindles were clamped. Each rocker and valve well was enclosed by its own polished, light-alloy, cover.

Ignition was by twin coils, fired by points set in the timing cover, which enclosed the camshaft drive gears. The points cam and its auto-advance were driven from the right-hand end of the inlet camshaft, and a small cover concealed the contact plate. The timing cover also enclosed the duplex-gear oil pump, which was mounted below the timing gears and driven by a worm on the right-hand end of the crankshaft. The lubrication system was dry-sump with an external oil tank and operated much as that of the larger twins. There was no timed engine breather, just a connection between the crankcase and the oil tank.

The primary transmission went on the left, a duplex chain driving a multi-plate clutch with three springs and a built-in shock absorber. A tensioner was provided to keep the chain under control. The chaincase comprised inner and outer castings, held together by a row of screws, the inner section being a separate part and not included with the left-hand crankcase casting. The Wipac alternator went inside the chaincase on the end of the crankshaft to supply the power for the six volt electric system.

The four-speed gearbox was built in unit with the engine and came from the AMC lightweight range of singles. The layshaft was placed to the rear of the mainshaft, but in most respects the design followed the traditional British path. An inner cover supported the right-hand end of both shafts, and an outer one concealed the positive-stop mechanism, clutch lift and kickstarter details, while

Assembling the first Norton built at the AMC Plumstead works, a 349 cc Navigator.

111

That first Plumstead Norton on the assembly line, a standard version of the 350.

blending in with the timing cover.

The complete engine unit was carried in a frame built up from a variety of pressed and tubular members, and based firmly on that of a Francis-Barnett, another AMC subsidiary. The frame had a pressed-steel member for a downtube, to which the headstock was welded, a central pressing, and two tubular loops. Rear suspension was by pivoted fork, and there were AMC lightweight telescopic forks at the front. Both full-width hubs also came from the Francis-Barnett and housed 6 in. single-leading-shoe brakes. They were spoked into 18 in. steel rims, each fitted with a 3.25 in. section tyre.

A major feature of the Jubilee was its rear enclosure, which was later taken up by the De Luxe versions of the larger twins. It comprised a rear section, with detachable number plate section, and side panels, each held by three fasteners. A deeply valanced front mudguard was fitted, and the oil tank, tool tray and electrics went beneath the dualseat.

The fixtures and fittings were conventional lightweight, so the control lever pivots were welded into place and the headlamp was a 6 in. one. The finish was two-tone with red, forest green or Tunisian blue for the upper tank, forks, headlamp and upper rear enclosure, while the lower tank and enclosure, front mudguard, frame and other details were in dove grey. The dualseat was in grey with a checked top.

Out on the road, the Jubilee was soon found to have an engine that needed to be revved to make it perform, and even then the actual performance was somewhat modest. Handling was acceptable, but the brakes were somewhat pressed to cope with the weight. The electrics were poor, with weak horn and lights, while the ignition timing would soon vary from its setting.

Oil leaks were a further problem, caused by the elementary breather and narrow joint faces. The engine was noisier than it should have been to fit its touring image and, being a twin, it vibrated when revved enough to produce acceptable power. The high engine speed also proved excessive for the large main bearings, which tended to skid instead of roll, wearing out too quickly. Shades of Commando problems to come, but not for the same reasons.

In all, the Jubilee did not get off to the best of starts, and the word soon spread that it was not the machine for the learner or novice. It continued into 1960 with minimal alterations, but much more happened for 1961.

The single model range became four for 1961 with the addition of the 349 cc Navigator and of standard versions in both capacities, but minus the rear enclosure. The Navigator engine was based firmly on the Jubilee, but was stretched to 63 x 56 mm dimensions. Internally, there was a steel crankshaft, while the two cylinders were combined into one block to increase the rigidity of the engine structure. The cylinder heads remained separate, while the carburettor bore was increased to 7/8 in.

The Navigator frame was similar to that of the Jubilee, but had a strengthened down-member. At the front went the Roadholder forks and the full-width hub with 8 in. brake from the larger twins. This was spoked into a 19 in. rim carrying a 3.00 in. section tyre. In other respects, the Navigator copied the smaller twin, and both were listed as de luxe models.

The standard versions of the two twins lost the rear enclosure and deep mudguard valance, having regular guards fitted in their place. The centre pressing was amended to offer a styling line and had side panels fitted to it which filled the subframe corners on each side.

Various options appeared; flat handlebars, screen, legshields and panniers all joining the full chaincase that had

been listed from the start. In this way, the four models and their options ran on for 1962 and into 1963.

In January 1963 a fifth machine joined the others, but at first it was for export to America only. The new model was called the Electra 400, and its engine had been enlarged to 383 cc by boring out the Navigator unit to 66 mm, while the specification included 12 volt electrics, an electric starter and turn signals. The engine looked very similar to the others, but differed in the crankcase, block and crankshaft, all of which had to be altered to allow for the larger bore. There was also a revised, stronger, gearbox with a different selector and change mechanism.

A high-output alternator replaced the stock item and a second six volt battery joined the first to make up the 12 volts. This was for the benefit of the Lucas electric starter, which was mounted to the back of the primary chaincase behind the block. From there, it drove the crankshaft by chain and sprockets, with a further ratio reduction in a set of epicyclic gears housed in the starter end casting. The turn signals were fitted into the ends of the handlebars, so they could be damaged very easily, while their control switch was placed on the right-hand bar, not the best of positions. Conversely, the starter button went on the left-hand bar - again, not the best place.

The cycle parts of the Electra were generally as for the Navigator, except that the full-width rear hub with 7 in. brake from the larger models was fitted. The wheel and tyre sizes remained the same, but the finish was much more in the Norton tradition, with a silver grey tank, oil tank and toolbox, and the remainder in black. The mudguards were chrome-plated as standard but, when the model reached its home market later in the year, this was the optional finish; as standard, they were in black. The turn signals were also an option for the home

The 1963 Electra 400 with chrome-plated mudguards and the turn signals mounted in the ends of the handlebars.

market where the model was listed as the ES400.

Rear enclosure was dropped at the end of 1963, so only the standard versions of the Jubilee and Navigator continued, along with the Electra. Changes were few, but the flat bars became standard and the raised ones optional, while the rear number plate was widened to cater for a change in the registration mark system in the UK. The Roadholder forks, with legs at an increased centre distance and with a steering lock, were fitted to the two larger models. For the Electra, the chrome-plated mudguards were fitted as standard, as were the turn signals.

During 1964 the Electra gearbox became the standard and was fitted to the other two models. All three ran on as they were for 1965, and at the end of that season the two larger machines were dropped. This left the standard Jubilee for 1966, but it went, too, when AMC failed during that year.

Prospects

Not very good for these small twins, as they were never among the preferred Norton models. There is a group of en-thusiasts who enjoy them, and some have even managed to overcome the oil leaks with care and modern sealants. The larger models benefited from the Roadholder forks and proper Norton wheel, or wheels, and should be less prone to leaks, thanks to the more rigid structure resulting from the use of a block instead of two separate cylinders.

The de luxe models with their rear enclosure just about make three stars thanks to this feature, but only just for the Navigator and with even more of a struggle for the Jubilee. This puts the standard machines down to two stars with the same proviso, so the Jubilee is really more like one-and-a-half.

For the Electra, I think we can go back to three stars, even if the starter was never much good with a cold engine. The model benefits from having the better forks and wheels, while being less common and, thus, perhaps more collectable. Out on the road, either of the larger models will be better than the Jubilee, and the de luxe Navigator with rear enclosure has to be the better investment, but only if complete and in good order.

Chapter 9

Specials and moderns

★★★★★	any works racer
★★★★	1953 248 cc single
★★★★	1973 NVT P92
★★★★	1953 497 cc side-valve twin
★★★★★	1965 800 cc ohc twin
★★★★	1973 500 cc Wulf twin
★★★★	1976 829 cc Norton 76 twin
★★★★★	1975 747 cc Cosworth twin
★★★★★	1987 Classic
★★★★	1988 Commander
★★★★	1989 F1

A short chapter this, as none of these models really comes within the compass of a buyer's guide. However, it is useful to know what exists, where it may be, and how unlikely it is that it will ever reach the marketplace. The bulk of these machines are one-offs and will not be for sale. If you are offered one, first lock up your money, as the chances of it being real are extremely remote.

Follow these leads at your financial peril!

Works racers

One or two works Manx racers did leave the factory, as did one or two prototypes. All known are in museums and are not for sale. An example of this is the outside-flywheel 350, as campaigned by the works in 1954. Another is the F-type, which was designed as a horizontal single for 1955, but was never raced or fully completed by the works.

Slightly earlier was a kneeler solo model, dubbed the 'Silver Fish', which was raced once in 1953. It had a 350 cc engine fitted into a frame with lowered top rails and supplied with fuel from pannier tanks. The machine was fully streamlined with built-in kneeling recesses for the rider, so it was very low. It set a new lap record in its one race in which it retired! The Silver Fish was used once more in practice for the TT and was later run at Montlhéry where it broke many records, including the important one hour at 133.71 miles.

Singles

There are two of these, the first being of 248 cc with inclined engine and high camshaft. It was built in 1953 as a prototype, had the gearbox bolted to the back of the engine and used conventional cycle parts. It is now at Beaulieu - only one was made.

The second single came later and was typed the NVT P92. It was a real industry hybrid, for the engine was a BSA 499 cc B50 unit and the frame came from a Triumph Bandit (a model that failed to reach production). The two were put together using the Norton Isolastic principal as on the Commando. It was constructed in

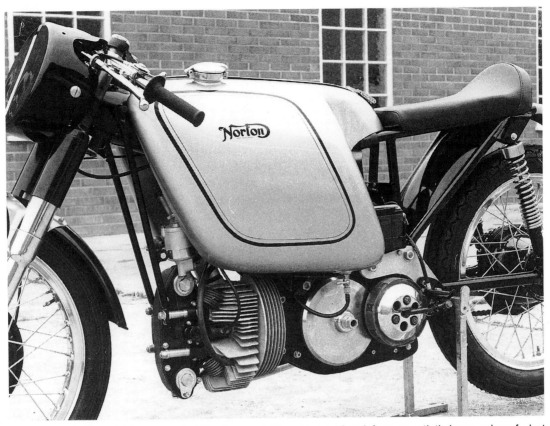

The horizontal, type F, Manx, as rebuilt by Sammy Miller with petrol tank from an artist's impression of what might have been.

1973 with various group detail parts to complete it and ran quite well for a prototype. At the time, this was not good enough, so no more was heard of it.

Twins

Rather more of these, the first being a one-off built in 1953 with a side-valve engine for the army. It was an attempt to replace the Triumph TRW twin, but never really had much chance of this due to the existing machine and spares holdings.

The machine used the Dominator engine with a new side-valve block and head. This worked well with the forward camshaft, so the rest of the engine was stock, other than the fitment of an alternator and coil ignition. As was done later on the standard machines, the ignition was controlled by a distributor mounted in the normal magneto position.

A cast-alloy chaincase enclosed the primary drive to the laid-down gearbox. The frame was from one of the rigid single-cylinder models and fitted with the Roadholder front forks, a 500T petrol tank, stock wheels and a saddle. The machine was built and demonstrated, but nothing further came of the project. Years later, it was restored by Sammy Miller for his museum where it now resides.

Next came the P10, which was a factory prototype of the mid-1960s. It had a twin-cylinder, 800 cc engine with twin overhead camshafts and a five-speed, unit-construction gearbox. The cylinders were inclined and the camshafts driven

116

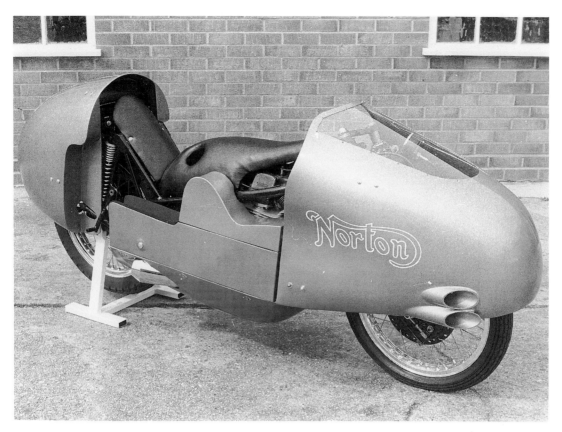

Restored kneeler Norton, known as the 'Silver Fish', which was raced just once, but broke world records.

by an excessively long chain, which ran through small tubes on the right-hand side of the engine.

This interesting engine was mounted in a modified Featherbed frame using mainly stock Norton cycle parts, but an AMC oil tank. Its performance failed to match that of the Atlas and, being a vertical twin, it suffered equally from vibration. For these, and other problems, the firm abandoned the P10 and went for the Commando with its proven engine and vibration-absorbing mounting system. The P10 now resides at the National Motorcycle Museum near Birmingham.

It was well into the 1970s before the next twin appeared - with a cross-pump, two-stroke engine, far removed from the usual Norton line. The machine was called the Wulf, and its engine looked much like any other air-cooled twin with the cylinders slightly inclined forward. Inside went two-diameter pistons, the ports being arranged to connect the lower annular volume on one side to the combustion space on the other. This design kept the mixture out of the crankcase altogether, which avoided many of the problems associated with the two-stroke.

The engine was built in unit with the gearbox, and the whole was fitted into a monocoque frame with slimline forks, disc front brake and detail fittings of the period. The Wulf was shown to the press, but then dropped from sight, only to resurface some years later with watercooling and reed valves. Little further was heard of it.

The P10 twin with overhead camshafts driven by a very long chain and now in the National Motorcycle Museum.

The last twin of this group was the Norton 76, which was an exercise with a Commando. It was nearly all stock Mk III, but had nice cast-alloy wheels with twin discs at the front and a special paint job. It is now in private hands.

Cosworth

In 1973, Norton commissioned Cosworth, the racing car engine firm, to produce a new 750 cc power unit suitable for both road and racing use. Behind the request lay the notion that this could be easily accomplished by taking two cylinders from the existing 3-litre Formula One engine. This presented the new unit with watercooling, twin overhead camshafts and a four-valve combustion chamber, all well-developed. The complete machine was to be called the Challenge.

The engine was inclined forward a little and built in unit with a five-speed gearbox. In the event, it turned out to be a complex unit, for it had twin balance shafts to inhibit the vibration and these had to be driven, along with the camshafts. This was done by combinations of toothed belt and spur gears, the camshafts opening the valves via bucket tappets.

A single main casting formed most of the crankcase plus the block, which had wet liners. The mains and big-ends were plain, and a heavy flywheel went in the centre of the crankshaft. The drive to the gearbox went via a quill shaft within the front balance shaft and then by inverted tooth chain to the clutch. The gearbox was all-indirect and could be built up and assembled to the main casting as a unit.

The cycle side of the Challenge was also innovative, the engine unit forming part of the frame structure. The suspension systems and other details were attached to it, and at the front went leading-link forks at first, but later these were changed to telescopics. At the rear, the fork was a cast-alloy structure which pivoted in the main engine casting with twin units to control it. Both wheels were cast-alloy with single discs, the rear one being mounted outboard of the fork leg on the sprocket side.

The Challenge ran at Brands Hatch late in 1975 and once or twice more, but was not competitive, being down on power and too heavy compared with the opposition. Cosworth themselves became far too busy with their car engine commitments to spare any time to deal with the engine, so the whole project came to an end.

Many years later, in 1985, the machines were privately revived for the Battle of the Twins racing class. In this, they were reasonably competitive and made a change from the usual run of models in the races.

Rotary engines

Around the middle 1970s, Norton inherited a rotary, or Wankel, engine project which reached them from Triumph, via the BSA group research centre at Umberslade Hall. Much of the work had been government-funded and progress was often slow, but development models

Wulf cross-pump, two-stroke twin on show and a far cry from the usual Norton machine.

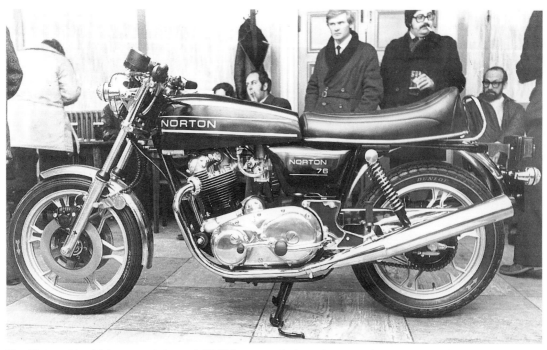

The Norton 76, which was mainly stock MkIII Commando, but with cast-alloy wheels and twin front discs.

were built and run in the late 1970s.

The project crawled into the 1980s with many launch dates postponed, although some machines were delivered to the police for their assessment. Others went to the services, this activity being enough to keep the financial wheels rolling and, in turn, enabling a watercooled version to be developed.

Finally, late in 1987, the civilian model was launched with the aircooled engine. It was called the Classic, but only a single batch of 100 machines was to be built. In the middle of 1988, watercooled models for both police and public were launched as the Commander, and the firm took up road racing once more, gaining a good deal of publicity due to their use of the rotary engine. This continued into 1989 when, once again, they were sponsored by John Player and had a successful season on British circuits. By the end of the year, one of their riders, Steve Spray, had

won two national championships, both by a good margin.

Late in 1988 the firm had shown a well streamlined and enclosed prototype sports version, labelled the P55. By early 1989 it was in JPS black with gold stripes and was officially launched late that year as the F1 roadster. It attracted a good deal of attention when shown and, with the Commander, looked set to carry the Norton name on into the 1990's.

More models were promised for 1991, a limited edition, watercooled Classic, a F1-JPS Special, a racing FIR, and the racing engine from the FIR for those who just wanted that unit. However, the recession and Norton's own financial problems prevented any of this happening. The Commander was joined by a version having the panniers permanently attached, both continuing with the expensive F1.

For 1992 the F1 Sports replaced the F1, at a reduced price, the Commanders ran

The Cosworth twin engine, on which Norton pinned some hopes in the early 1970s.

on, and Steve Hislop won the Senior TT for the firm. Despite this success, the firm was unable to capitalise on it, but did show the F2 prototype late in the year.

Sadly, their problems grew worse so that production ceased during 1993.

Police group with rotary-engined machines, one standard and the other with its full police equipment.

Prospects

Of getting your hands on most of the above, these are very slim. Few are going to come on the market again and, even if they do, they are likely to have been spoken for long ago. Thus, it may be five stars for the works Manx, the overhead camshaft twin, the Cosworth and the Classic, but only the last is a likely possible purchase.

The others have four stars, but are equally inaccessible, except for the up-to-the-minute Commander and F1. Both of these are likely to hold their value well, for they are unlikely to be built in large numbers. In some ways, their future is the hardest to predict.

The 1988 Commander with rotary engine which took Norton back into the market place.

Chapter 10

Looking and buying

The previous chapters have sought to tell you about the different Norton ranges and models so you know how they fit together, their extent and how they came and went. You now need to plan how to find what you seek, how to look it over and how to negotiate an acceptable price.

Nortons, especially Commando twins, were one of the most popular makes of the postwar era, and have continued in this role in the classic revival of the 1980s. While there are still plenty of singles about, there is little doubt that the majority of Nortons to be seen are twins, with Commandos outnumbering the older Featherbed types.

Wonderful if you can find one. Lovely camshaft single from the late 1930s, all there and ripe for a full restoration.

A nice machine to be wary of if buying, as it is actually a 1952-54 type frame fitted with a 1958 engine. Headlamp is 1956 and mudguards alloy.

This situation has been helped by the easy way in which many of the parts will interchange, although this, in turn, can bring problems. One of the tasks of this book is to help solve these problems by providing the buyer with the information he, or she, needs when viewing a prospect. However, don't forget that the seller, too, may have a copy, so always be on your guard.

Buying any motorcycle is a process of location, viewing and negotiation, best done in that order. At all stages, the more you know, the better the situation will be, regardless of what you are buying or from whom. A crisp remark that some feature cannot be original can work wonders for your self-confidence, but only if

you have the data to back it up should you be challenged.

Tact may also help, since some owners will not take kindly to any suggestion that their masterpiece could have feet of clay. Thus, the owner's temperament should be gauged while asking about the machine's history - or you could find yourself in the street. With the more desirable models, some owners will only sell to what they see as a good home, and set themselves up as judge and jury on this. As demand usually exceeds supply, there is no way round this if you want the machine, but invariably the owner will respond to your enthusiasm.

Norton twin from 1967 with minor owner changes which do not detract from the machine at all.

Determining your needs

Before you try to locate your Norton, you should first decide which model you want and what you will use it for. Sounds obvious, but all too often a machine is bought on impulse and within weeks is found not to fit the new owner's needs, wishes or pocket. It's much better to think it out first, even though many of the factors may conflict and chance can always bring the unexpected.

Your needs, if you intend to ride the machine on a daily basis, are a good deal different than those that apply if you wish to exhibit at shows. Between these two extremes are weekend use, regular rallies or occasional rides, and all affect your choice.

Anything approaching regular use suggests that you will need to sacrifice originality for better brakes, lights, tyres and suspension. All can be altered with-

out losing that typical Norton line, and for many owners this gives a most desirable result. They finish up with the marque they want, but updated and amended to use modern technology to keep pace with modern traffic. This is a philosophy from the postwar era, when it was common practice for machines to be modified to improve them, update them or simply adapt them to their owner's need.

In some cases, the changes became major, with the Featherbed Norton frame providing the base for many a special, the Triton being the most common. This combined the easily-tuned Triumph twin engine with the frame to produce a classic which was still in demand and being built as new in the 1980s. The frame was also used with many other engines, but not in anything like the numbers of the Triton, which remained the classic de-

A 1972 Interpol could take your fancy, but be careful about road use, as impersonating a police officer is not on.

sign.

The Triton reflects one builder's personal needs, so in any form it can be regarded as being in original condition. Not so a standard model, and to the restorer and concours exhibitor original fitments are all-important. With the rapid growth of the classic movement, this has brought its own set of problems, for some parts that turn up are new-old-stock (NOS) and, thus, genuine, even if ancient. Others are reproduction parts and their quality can vary greatly. If internal parts, they may affect reliability, while if external, they may alter the appearance. Carburettors, exhaust systems, tank and footrest rubbers, transfers and tyres are all items that wear or deteriorate, so are likely to need replacement. Somehow, to the experienced eye, reproduction parts always look like reproductions, even in a photograph.

Your intended use will indicate the model and era that you should seek, but this will always be subject to what you can afford. For many of us, this may mean an adjustment, and we may have to settle for a 16H or Jubilee rather than the International or John Player Commando we crave. Once you have got over the initial disappointment, you'll realize that it's better to own a machine you can really afford than one that will stretch your resources to breaking point.

The amount you spend to purchase the machine is never the end, as there are always further costs with any motorcycle. How much depends on the condition of the machine and the alterations you plan to make. A no-expense-spared restoration job can run into a large sum if you farm out the work, and a sizable one even when you do much of the work yourself. Do not take on more than your workshop or abilities can cope with, and do not delude yourself on this point. If you do, you can easily pull the machine apart and get stuck, then find you cannot afford the services of a specialist and have to dispose of the resultant basket case at a loss. Set your sights at an attainable level and accept that you may not have the facilities or skills to do it all. Few of us have.

All this must be taken into account, and you should plan to leave yourself enough money after the purchase to cover tax, insurance and any needed work. The last item will always come to twice your estimate.

Gaining knowledge

Before you start hunting for your machine, find out as much about it as you can. You are holding a good deal of what you need in your hand right now, so read it before you go shopping, not afterwards. That way, you can be assured that you are getting the best buy to suit you.

It is important that you keep this last point in mind, and buy for your needs and not someone else's. Ignore them and concentrate on yourself, for if you are happy with your machine, it is of no account what others may think of your choice.

Add to your knowledge by checking the prices of both private and dealer machines, making notes on their condition. You will soon learn that they come in many forms, ranging from the bare bones at an autojumble or swop meet to a concours restoration job bought from a specialist dealer. Machines may be original or not, complete or not, shabby, rusty or partly restored. They can be badly restored, which may be worse, as there may be untold horrors under the covers.

Build up your store of knowledge so that you can begin to make a reasonably accurate assessment of most models and conditions. That way, you should buy at

This is a famous old Norton known as 'Old Miracle', so it will not be for sale. It dates from 1912 and broke many records at that time.

Engine of an early 1920s 16H with that familiar Norton line.

the right price, unless you let your heart rule your head. Fight this, if you can, so at least you keep to a sensible price, if not the best one.

Locating the machine

The possible sources for finding the right machine are dealers, small advertisements in local papers and specialized magazines, auctions, local and one-make clubs, autojumbles and personal contacts. All need to be followed up, especially if you are after a rare model. Few Manx Nortons come on to the open market, for most already have a queue of potential buyers who have asked the owner for first refusal.

The expensive solution is a dealer who specialises in either Nortons or vintage and classic machines. These days, you are not likely to find a machine at a general bike shop at anything less than the going rate, and often it will be more expensive than usual because the dealer has heard vaguely that all such machines are now worth real money.

Small advertisements present two problems. One is that the worthwhile

A nicely restored Manx on show with a BSA Rocket 3 in the 1970s.

machines always seem to be a long distance away. The other problem is establishing the real condition before you set out on the journey. All too often, the owner's glowing description is a bit exaggerated and the machine turns out to be too rusty, too incomplete or too poorly restored to make it a good proposition.

Even if you have travelled all day, the golden rule is to keep your money in your pocket unless you really are happy with what is on offer. We have all done the opposite more than once, but invariably pangs of regret will set in halfway through the return journey or soon after the mistake has been installed in your garage.

In this circumstance, it may be worth making a silly offer. Before you open your mouth, make two positive decisions. One is to ask yourself if you want the machine at all, even if it was free. Do not

kid yourself that it will be handy for spares, because it won't be. All the parts you are likely to need because your main machine is in trouble will also be worn out, split or otherwise useless. It is possible that the offering may have parts on it that you could use, but only allow for the price of those parts and nothing else. Remember, they are bound to need some repair and maybe repainting.

The second decision is the amount at which to pitch your silly offer. Decide on two figures, the first being your opening offer and the second being the maximum amount you are prepared to go to. If the owner says 'No way' to your offers, just drive home and start hunting again.

Auctions can offer a wide selection of machines and conditions. You can look and read the description in the catalogue, but you can't run the engine. Check

The type of machine advertised as an easy restoration, as it is all there and not in bad condition. Machine is a 1961 650SS

carefully that the machine corresponds to its description and really is what you seek, because there will be no going back. Listen to the auctioneer at the start to establish sales conditions and if there is a buyer's premium. Decide on your limit before the auction starts, write it in the catalogue and stick to it regardless. If the machine fails to reach its reserve, seek out the owner to see if you can strike a deal. After all, he or she will not have to pay commission and will hardly wish to trail the model back home again.

The local club is unlikely to provide much of a selection of machines, but you might find a bargain. Make sure both you and the seller are interested in dealing, though. If the seller is hesitant, but you're not, the deal could cost you more in the long run. The one-make club may be a better bet. There will be more on

offer, with the chance of finding some nice machines at the right price and with a decent history behind them. The Norton club in the UK produces its own magazine entitled Roadholder, while the equivalent in the USA is the International Norton Owner's Association who have their own newsletter. Both can be a good source of machines and parts.

Autojumbles and swop meets can be a source of complete machines, but be extra careful, since there will be no comeback. Most machines on offer will be tired and well worn, often with a fair number of items missing. Some will have engines that do not match their frames, and internals not belonging to their externals. Occasionally, you will find a machine that is original, essentially complete and worth considering. The stall holder will know what it is worth, so there will not be much room for bargaining, but always make the attempt.

Most purchases at autojumbles consist of parts or assemblies, but even these need some careful checking. It is for this purpose that I wrote *Norton Twin Restoration*, with its up-to-the-elbows detail, and it will also help with the cycle parts of some of the singles. Check, check and check again, and someday you may find a 'swan' under the rust and grime - but not often.

Personal contacts can be best of all. In some cases, they may be your only lead to finding the rare models, so the more you have, the better your chances. While perseverance is fine, always remember to keep to the right side of the fine line between keeping in contact and becoming a nuisance and a bore.

Even trickier is the situation where the owner, usually a man, dies to leave a widow with a desirable machine. It is hardly proper etiquette to make your bid at the graveside, but fatal to wait too long, otherwise another will succeed in your place. The matter of price can also be awkward, for the widow may not know or care as to the machine's value. Often, a son, close relative or friend will take charge of the disposal of the machine and other relevant items, which, at least, makes it easier to conduct business.

Basket cases

Basket cases are best left alone unless you know a great deal about Nortons, in which case the warning is superfluous. In theory, the various boxes shown to you will contain one complete motorcycle, dismantled into its component parts. In practice, the machine may have been incomplete even when the parts were together.

It is far more likely that the parts come from more than one model, often other marques as well, and will never make a complete machine. There are exceptions, but they do not occur often and the trick is to recognise one when it appears. It is also usual for the parts to be well worn, and often the result of a garage or workshop clear-out where the owner has had a series of similar models, and what is on

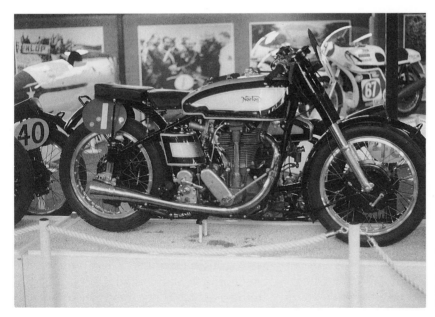

After restoration, an early postwar Manx on show at the National Motorcyle Museum.

Not to everyone's taste, but a nice picture of a 1963 Electra 400 with standard mudguard finish and without the turn signals

offer are the discards.

Basket cases can better be viewed as a box of spares that may be useful and must be priced accordingly. Even where the seller is quite genuine about the machine and its history, it is all too easy to forget items that were missing or broken or lent to a friend. Keep well clear unless you are certain or have an expert to advise and assist you with the deal and the assembly.

Viewing the bike

Some people have this down to a fine art and, with a few well chosen phrases, can imply that they are doing the seller a favour by removing the machine and really ought to be paid for this kindness.

Most of us find the going harder, but with any classic it is an essential stage.

The job depends greatly on the condition of the machine in the general sense, as this sets the standards to be looked for. A machine with rounded nuts, dull paint work, dangling cables and an unkempt air is unlikely to be mechanically perfect inside, so should be judged on that basis. A decent exterior usually implies that the interior is similar, and also that it is correct for the model. Even where the outside has been spruced up in an attempt to mask an indifferent condition, it is usually fairly easy to spot this with a little practice. There will be too much polish on the main covers, none in the recesses and not enough correct settings and adjustments.

The parameters to use when viewing depend on the use to which you will put the machine, as has been discussed already. Do not forget these, otherwise you could end up with the wrong machine at the wrong price. However, whether the machine is for daily riding or weekend showing, the state of completeness, correctness and condition all count. The degree to which they count will vary according to use, but in all cases a nice machine is worth having and a wreck is always a wreck.

There are basic inspection checks to be made when looking over any machine with a view to buy, and these apply regardless of model, originality or type, so always need to be carried out. Start with the overview, to assess whether it is more or less all there, the general condition and whether it still excites you or produces a feeling of dread. If the latter, then say farewell and go on your way. You will never be happy with it, even after an expensive rebuild.

Next, check it in detail from stem to stern. Inspect the tyres, try to rock the wheels and feel how they turn, look for play in front and rear suspension, see if the headstock is tight or loose once the damper is slack, and check the suspension for movement, noise and damping.

Look over the cycle parts for splits and cracks, as these will need welding and then refinishing. See if there are dents in the tanks, since these could be expensive to correct, inspect the underside of the petrol tank for signs of leaks or attempts to mend same. See if the brakes work at

A potential investment is this limited-edition Classic model with aircooled rotary engine.

Features of the Commando S model of 1969-70 were the headlamp protector ring and forks without gaiters.

all and whether the spokes need replacement. Check the controls and switches to see if they work easily and correctly or are either stiff and corroded or sloppy and worn out.

Finally, check the engine and gearbox. Look over both for oil leaks, signs of excess jointing compound and cracked or broken fins or lugs. See if the chains are in good order and adjustment, and then ask the owner to start the machine. If you receive a refusal or a feeble excuse, either be on your way or drastically revise your opening offer. There is no reason why any Norton should not start easily and run nicely. Learn how they sound before you go shopping so you have a good idea of what you should hear.

Expect first gear to engage quietly when the machine is at a standstill and for the drive to take up smoothly. The gears should change quickly and easily, so if they don't there is either a gearbox problem or the clutch needs attention. Be wary of riding a machine with any indication of gearbox trouble.

If you do ride the machine on the road, or as a passenger, expect it to run in a happy manner. They normally do, so if you find one that does not, this indicates a need for some adjustment as a minimum, and maybe some major work. Even if it is only a matter of a minor correction, the fact that the seller has not bothered is a clear indication of attitude. While out

Production Racer Commando which was very successful in its day, and they still run well in classic events.

The Mk 2 model 50 and ES2 of 1965-66 were AMC products with Norton badges and deserved the poor reception they received.

on the road, try to see if the wheels run in line as they should, as this could indicate trouble or confirm a good buy if all is well.

Identification

In addition to the general checks, there are more specific ones as well as paperwork, which come together in some cases. Start with the engine and frame numbers which MUST be taken from the machine and MUST be checked against those shown in the registration document. In the UK this is called the V5, and if one is not forthcoming it may well be that the machine is not registered and not entitled to the number plate it carries.

These numbers must be checked, otherwise there could be problems in the future. In the UK, if there is no V5, you will have to apply for one, supplying proof of ownership of the machine and a dating letter to confirm the age of the model. If all is well, it will be issued with an age-related mark; if not, it will receive

a number with a letter Q prefix. Either will devalue it to a degree in its home country where the original number is often held in high esteem, but procedures in other countries differ.

The next stage is to compare the numbers with those given in the appendices of this book, bearing in mind that the model year runs from the previous August. Thus, a 1955 model, for example, could be built, sold and then registered in late 1954. Check out the year letter, model code and the actual number on both engine and frame, remembering that for most postwar machines these should be the same.

The above tells you what the machine should be, but you need to confirm that it is what it claims to be. For this, use the identity charts given in the appendices to check out the external features for the model in question. If any feature is not there, or is not as it should be, look through the charts to see which model it has come from. Where necessary, refer also to the general text, but in most cases the chart should cover all that you can inspect of a complete machine.

The internals are another matter, but if the outside checks out, there is a good chance that the interior will also. However, always remember that it is only too easy to change parts around in the twin, so be extra careful with the sports models. Not that it is all that desirable to find SS cams in an early model 7, as the all-iron engine may well protest, as will an iron head on a real SS engine.

One further check can be the finish and colours, which are also given in the appendices. The patina of age on an original finish can be detected quite easily, as can a new coat of paint. If the colours do not check out, this may not be too serious, but it is another factor to take into account with your overall assessment.

If the machine is not all standard, you have to decide how important this is to you, which will depend on your intended use. For general riding, it will not matter much and the changes may well be desir-able improvements. If you are going to show the machine, however, they can be more important, and in this case a judgment has to be made as to the effect and the ease of correction. Some detail parts may be simple enough to replace with originals, but others could prove impossible.

Negotiations

These can be short or protracted. It may be a case of agreeing a price without negotiation, or a conversation that continues for months before a deal is finally struck. Fortunately, for most of us, the middle course prevails and an equitable price is arrived at without too much delay.

There is no negotiation in the normal sense at an auction, where you have to decide on your limit and stick to it. Only if the machine fails to reach its reserve are you likely to be able to do a private deal.

When buying from a dealer or a private owner, there will normally be a stated asking price. This may be viewed as a starting point and represents the highest

Restored 1947 Manx out in California and showing its drive-side.

137

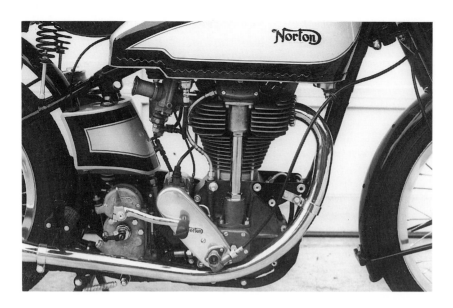

Timing-side and engine of the 1947 Manx - not easy to get as good as this one.

Very nice flat-tank Norton with period sidecar seen at the 1989 Banbury run. A fine example to us all.

Navigator de luxe from 1962 with its rear enclosure, Roadholder forks and large front brake.

value the owner has dared to pitch without running the risk of losing all response to his advert or whatever. This may state that the price is not negotiable, but most are, especially when the seller is faced with a pile of crisp bank notes.

The price may have the letters 'ono' or 'ovno' alongside it, which stand for 'or near offer' or 'or very near offer' and indicate that the owner is prepared to barter to an extent. How much may often be gauged from the figure. Thus '£650 ono' most likely means that £600 would be highly acceptable and maybe as much as was really expected. On the other hand, '£650 ovno' means you may offer £600, but will probably settle at the split on £625. A quick survey of a recent magazine will give many more examples of this type.

Just as the asking price is the highest that the seller hopes to get, so your first offer is the lowest you will be able to buy at. Think long and hard before coming out with a figure, for it will be nearly impossible to reduce it later. The only chance of this is if some undisclosed fact comes to light during the discussion. But even this will not do much to strengthen your position.

First ask yourself whether you really want the model, whether it fits your needs and if the one you are looking at is the right machine. It may be fitted with a number of options which the seller will claim greatly enhances its value and, while this may be true, they only count if you really want them.

If you finally decide that you have found just the machine for you, then run through your notes for faults to criticize and features that are non-standard or unwanted. Work out the figure you could be happy at and then go down to your first silly offer.

This may be greeted with derision, but it is a start and the ball is now with the seller, who can either say 'no way', or suggest another figure. Keep at it, but remember that you may not be alone in reading these words!

The deal

All being well, you should arrive at a price with the seller in due course. This may involve a trade-in with a dealer, although this is less usual with the older machines, and your calculations must take all this into account.

Once you have paid for the machine, it

A Manx Norton in use, most likely in practice for a TT or the Manx GP in the mid-1950s, when the model dominated many events

is your responsibility, which means you need to insure it. Even if you do not intend to ride it on the road immediately, you should cover it against fire and theft. It will be best to go to a specialist broker who can arrange coverage on an 'agreed value' basis to reflect what the model is worth. The coverage for road use may also be on a restricted mileage basis, which will be more suited to the use that most owners will have in mind.

When you pay for the machine, do get a receipt that details the machine, registration mark and engine and frame numbers. Also, in the UK, collect the V5 and MoT documents, if there are any, and any other material on the machine, such as parts list, owner's handbook or instruction manual. Check that they are relevant to the model and year; if not, they will need replacement.

The next problem you will face is transporting the machine home, since you can ride it only if all the documentation is in order and you have your riding gear with you. Often, it will mean using a van or a car and trailer, unless the seller can assist.

THE GOLDEN RULE

If you are not totally happy about the machine, leave it to someone else and walk away. Make sure you know what 'totally happy' means for you, regardless of others' opinions of the machine's value or investment rating. If the machine really is the one you want, then buy it and enjoy it to the full, whether Manx or 16H, Commando or Jubilee.

Nice Dunstall Dominator with high-level pipes, tank, seat, tail unit and fittings supplied by
Paul. Very tasty.

Perhaps an investment for the future, the F1 of 1990 with its rotary engine and high
purchase price.

Engine and frame numbers

From 1945 to 1974 these should match, and up to 1960 should include a year letter code. There will also be a number code for the model, and the serial number which ran from 1001 to over 300,000 over the years.

The engine number is stamped on the left-hand crankcase just below the cylinder and may include the engine dimensions, especially on the singles with the 79 x 100 mm bore and stroke. The frame number may be on the headstock, but Featherbed frames are numbered on the left-hand rear frame gusset, above the fork pivot. Normally the serial number is in a vertical line with the year and model codes above it. Commando frames are numbered on a plate riveted to the headstock. The small twins, such as the Jubilee, have their frame number stamped on the right-hand frame lug which carried the rear fork up to 1963. From then on, it went on the pillion footrest bracket.

There was some overlap of numbers from one model year, or calendar year, to the next, so the year code letter is more useful up to 1960. Therefore, the serial numbers given are approximate and relate to the year's end.

Note that there are exceptions and, thus, there is known to exist a 1946 ES2 with letter A year code, even though the model was not re-introduced until 1947.

The year code letters are :

A	1946	F	1951	L	1956
B	1947	G	1952	M	1957
C	1948	H	1953	N	1958
D	1949	J	1954	P	1959
E	1950	K	1955	R	1960

The model codes are :

2	16H	122	88
3	18	13	50
3T	500T	14	99
4	ES2	15	77 & Nomad
6	19R	16	Nomad
7	Big 4	17	Jubilee
8	16H or Big 4 plunger	18	all 650 twins
9	19S	19	Navigator
10	International 40	20	Atlas
10M	Manx 40	20M3	Commando
10M2	Manx 40		(distributor)
	Featherbed	20M3S	Commando
11	International 30		(camshaft
11M	Manx 30		points)
11M2	Manx 30	50	AMC 50
	Featherbed	ES	Electra
12	Model 7	ES2	AMC ES2

Suffix D indicates de luxe twin
Suffix SS indicates Sports Special twin
Suffix Q indicates quietening ramp cams
(some 1947 singles)

Serial numbers for engine and frame :

1945	1001	1956	66600	1967	119760
1946	2131	1957	71360	1968	124300
1947	7756	1958	77400	1969	130000
1948	13792	1959	80488	1970	134700
1949	20701	1960	87038	1971	141700
1950	27100	1961	94500	1972	200001
1951	35560	1962	101060	1973	212278
1952	42700	1963	105000	1973	300000 (850)
1953	48900	1964	108000	1974	307311
1954	55350	1965	111650	1975	325000 (MkIII)
1955	60700	1966	115870		125001 (frame)

Electra July 1963	650
Sept. 1964	6201
Aug. 1965	7961

The F2 prototype on show at the NEC late in 1992. Its number plate reflects the Senior TT win of that year.

Norton identity and model range charts

The identity charts detail external features and are provided as a guide and check list when viewing a potential purchase. Engine and frame numbers remain the first points to check always, but the features can give a very good indication as to whether the machine is what it is said to be or is from another year or a hybrid.

The list of features for each model was first developed in an attempt to isolate a unique set for each year as a basis for checking. Many items appear for several models, as they were common to the range, but are included each time where they will help. The list was then expanded a little to include points that are often of interest, even when they may not help with dating. This may mean that for one particular year there are several points that changed, but all are included, as all should be there if the machine is original.

All the features listed are external ones which can be checked without dismantling. The internal changes are of no help when you are looking, but remember that they may be far reaching due to the ease with which parts may be switched around among models in some ranges. When going to view, make a list of points to check, but take the book, as it will help establish the source of any rogue parts.

The model range charts are derived automatically from the identity charts that give the years for which each model was built. These are also covered in the rating box at the beginning of each machine range chapter, and all are for the model year rather than the calendar year. The new season's models were built from August on, to be ready for the November show and distribution to the dealers, hence the distinction.

348 cc 40M & 490 cc 30M Manx

Feature	'46	'47	'48	'49	'50
plunger frame	*	*	*	*	*
telescopics	*	*	*	*	*
saddle & pad	*	*	*	*	*
21 in. front, 20 in. rear	*	*	*	*	*
dohc				*	*
alloy tanks				*	*

Featherbed Manx 30M & 40M

Feature	'51	'52	'53	'54	'55	'56	'57	'58	'59	'60	'61	'62	'63
Featherbed frame	*	*	*	*	*	*	*	*	*	*	*	*	*
welded subframe		*	*	*	*	*	*	*	*	*	*	*	*
short-stroke engine		*	*	*	*	*	*	*	*	*	*	*	*
fins - bevel shaft		*	*	*	*	*	*	*	*	*	*	*	*
coarse-pitch bevels						*	*	*	*	*	*	*	*
needle-roller shaft									*	*	*	*	*
rotating magnet mag					*	*	*	*	*	*	*	*	*
GP carburettor		*	*	*	*	*	*	*	*				
GP2 carburettor											*	*	*
weir float						*	*	*	*	*	*	*	*
reverse-cone (350)				*	*	*	*	*	*	*	*	*	*
fluted megaphone										*	*	*	*
megaphone clip stop											*	*	*
Renold chain oiler						*	*	*	*	*	*	*	*
laid-down gearbox	*	*	*	*	*	*	*						
AMC gearbox								*	*	*	*	*	*
gear lever strut						*	*	*	*	*	*	*	*
revised gear pedal										*	*	*	*
int. fork springs	*	*	*	*	*								
ext. fork springs						*	*	*	*	*	*	*	*
8 in. 2ls front brake				*	*	*	*	*	*	*			
7 in. dual 2ls front												*	*
glassfibre seat										*	*	*	*
oil tank rubber bands											*	*	*
welded-on lever pivots						*	*	*	*	*	*	*	*

International 30 & 40

Feature	'47	'48	'49	'50	'51	'52	'53	'54	'55	'56	'57	'58
plunger frame	*	*	*	*	*	*						
Featherbed frame							*	*	*	*	*	*
welded subframe									*	*	*	*
iron engine	*	*	*	*	*	*						
alloy engine							*	*	*	*	*	*
pear-shaped silencer							*	*	*	*		
tubular silencer											*	*
laid-down gearbox							*	*	*	*	*	*
21 in. front, 20 in. rear	*	*	*	*	*	*						
19 in. wheels							*	*	*	*	*	*
full-width hubs									*	*	*	*
8 in. front brake							*	*	*	*	*	*
saddle	*	*	*	*	*	*						
dualseat							*	*	*	*	*	*
underslung pilot							*	*	*			
wrap around oil tank	*	*	*	*	*	*						

ES2

Feature	'47	'48	'49	'50	'51	'52	'53	'54	'55	'56	'57	'58
revised timing case		*	*	*	*	*	*	*	*	*	*	*
alloy head									*	*	*	*
integral pushrod tunnel											*	*
Monobloc carb									*	*	*	*
pear-shaped silencer							*	*	*	*		
tubular silencer											*	*
laid-down gearbox				*	*	*	*	*	*	*		
AMC gearbox											*	*
plunger frame	*	*	*	*	*	*						
s/a frame							*	*	*	*	*	*
all-tubular frame											*	*
8 in. front brake							*	*	*	*	*	*
full-width hubs										*	*	*
alloy front backplate					*	*	*	*	*	*	*	*
revised oil tank										*	*	*
instrument panel										*		
shell with instruments											*	*
tank side panels											*	*
boxed rear no. plate									*	*	*	*
dualseat							*	*	*	*	*	*
underslung pilot							*	*	*			

ES2

Feature	'59	'60	'61	'62	'63
revised timing case	*	*	*	*	*
alloy head	*	*	*	*	*
integral pushrod tunnel	*	*	*	*	*
AC electrics	*	*	*	*	*
coil ignition	*	*	*	*	*
Monobloc carb	*	*	*	*	*
tubular silencer	*	*	*	*	*
engine plate cover	*	*	*	*	*
AMC gearbox	*	*	*	*	*
Featherbed frame	*	*	*	*	*
slimline frame			*	*	*
8 in. front brake	*	*	*	*	*
full-width hubs	*	*	*	*	*
alloy front backplate	*	*	*	*	*
revised oil tank	*	*	*	*	*
shell with instruments	*	*	*	*	*
tank side panels	*	*			
long tank badges			*	*	*
boxed rear no. plate	*	*	*	*	*
rear chaincase option	*	*	*	*	*

ES2Mk2 and 50Mk2

Feature	'65	'66
AMC engine	*	*
Norton forks	*	*
Norton wheels	*	*
AMC frame	*	*
AMC gearbox	*	*

348/490 Trials

Feature	'47	'48
listed	*	*

16H, 18 and Big 4

Feature	'45	'46	'47	'48	'49	'50	'51	'52	'53	'54
girder forks	*	*								
633 cc Big 4			*							
597 cc Big 4				*	*	*	*	*	*	*
revised timing case				*	*	*	*	*	*	*
sv alloy valve case				*	*	*	*	*	*	*
sv alloy head				*	*	*	*	*	*	*
laid-down gearbox						*	*	*	*	*
8 in. front brake										*
alloy front backplate							*	*	*	*
dualseat									*	*
underslung pilot									*	*

19R

Feature	'55
alloy head	*
Monobloc carb	*
pear-shaped silencer	*
laid-down gearbox	*
s/a frame	*
8 in. front brake	*
alloy front backplate	*
boxed rear no. plate	*
dualseat	*
underslung pilot	*

19S

Feature	'55	'56	'57	'58
as for ES2 plus	*	*	*	*
pear-shaped silencer	*	*		
tubular silencer			*	*
laid-down gearbox	*	*		
AMC gearbox			*	*
instrument panel			*	
shell with instruments			*	*
tank side panels			*	*
underslung pilot	*			

50

Feature	'56	'57	'58	'59	'60	'61	'62	'63
as for ES2 plus	*	*	*	*	*	*	*	*
Monobloc carb	*	*	*	*	*	*	*	*
pear-shaped silencer	*							
tubular silencer		*	*	*	*	*	*	*
laid-down gearbox	*							
AMC gearbox		*	*	*	*	*	*	*
s/a frame	*	*	*					
Featherbed frame				*	*	*	*	*
slimline frame						*	*	*
instrument panel	*							
shell with instruments		*	*	*	*	*	*	*
tank side panels		*	*	*	*			
long tank badges						*	*	*
AC electrics				*	*	*	*	*
coil ignition				*	*	*	*	*
engine plate cover				*	*	*	*	*
rear chaincase option				*	*	*	*	*

500T

Feature	'49	'50	'51	'52	'53	'54
listed	*	*	*	*	*	*
upright gearbox	*	*	*	*	*	*
special forks	*	*	*	*	*	*

Model 7

Feature	'49	'50	'51	'52	'53	'54	'55
plunger frame	*	*	*	*			
s/a frame					*	*	*
alloy head							*
Monobloc							*
21 in. front wheel	*	*	*	*			
19 in. front wheel					*	*	*
laid-down gearbox	*	*	*	*	*	*	*
saddle	*	*	*	*			
dualseat					*	*	*
pear-shaped silencer					*	*	*
oil gauge in tank	*	*	*	*			
8 in. front brake						*	*
alloy front backplate			*	*	*	*	*
underslung pilot					*	*	*

Model 88

Feature	'52	'53	'54	'55	'56	'57	'58	'59	'60	'61	'62	'63
alloy head				*	*	*	*	*	*	*	*	*
Monobloc				*	*	*	*	*	*	*	*	*
alternator							*	*	*	*	*	*
coil ignition							*	*	*	*	*	*
pear-shaped silencer	*	*	*	*	*							
tubular silencer							*	*	*	*	*	*
laid-down gearbox	*	*	*	*	*							
AMC gearbox							*	*	*	*	*	*
Featherbed frame	*	*	*	*	*	*	*	*	*	*	*	*
slimline frame									*	*	*	*
welded subframe				*	*	*	*	*	*	*	*	*
8 in. front brake			*	*	*	*	*	*	*	*	*	*
full-width hubs				*	*	*	*	*	*	*	*	*
tank side panels							*	*	*			
long tank badges									*	*	*	*
instrument panel					*							
shell with instruments							*	*	*	*	*	*
underslung pilot	*	*	*	*								
round footrests							*	*	*	*	*	*
chaincase option									*	*	*	*

Model 99

Feature	'56	'57	'58	'59	'60	'61	'62
alloy head	*	*	*	*	*	*	*
Monobloc	*	*	*	*	*	*	*
alternator			*	*	*	*	*
coil ignition			*	*	*	*	*
pear-shaped silencer	*						
tubular silencer		*	*	*	*	*	*
laid-down gearbox	*						
AMC gearbox		*	*	*	*	*	*
Featherbed frame	*	*	*	*	*	*	*
slimline frame					*	*	*
welded subframe	*	*	*	*	*	*	*
8 in. front brake	*	*	*	*	*	*	*
full-width hubs	*	*	*	*	*	*	*
tank side panels		*	*	*			
long tank badges					*	*	*
instrument panel	*						
shell with instruments		*	*	*	*	*	*
round footrests		*	*	*	*	*	*
chaincase option			*	*	*	*	

650

Feature	'61	'62	'63
slimline frame	*	*	*

88 & 99 de luxe

Feature	'60	'61	'62
slimline frame	*	*	*
rear enclosure	*	*	*

650 de luxe

Feature	'62
slimline frame	*
rear enclosure	*

88SS

Feature	'61	'62	'63	'64	'65	'66
twin carbs	*	*	*	*	*	*
downdraught inlet		*	*	*	*	*
coil ignition	*					
magneto ignition		*	*	*	*	*
12 volt electrics				*	*	*
wider forks				*	*	*
steering lock				*	*	*
3/8 in. rear chain					*	*

99SS

Feature	'61	'62
twin carbs	*	*
coil ignition	*	*

Model 77

Feature	'57	'58
s/a frame	*	*
596 cc engine	*	*
tubular silencer	*	*
8 in. front brake	*	*
AMC gearbox	*	*

650SS

Feature	'62	'63	'64	'65	'66	'67	'68	'69	'70
twin carbs	*	*	*	*	*	*	*		
Monobloc	*	*	*	*	*				
Concentric						*	*	*	*
magneto ignition	*	*	*	*	*				
capacitor ignition						*	*	*	*
12 volt electrics			*	*	*	*	*	*	*
wider forks			*	*	*	*	*	*	*
3/8 in. rear chain			*	*	*	*	*	*	*
seat hump							*	*	*
Mercury								*	*

Atlas

Feature	'62	'63	'64	'65	'66	'67	'68
front breather	*	*	*	*	*	*	*
single carb	*	*					
twin carbs			*	*	*	*	*
Monobloc	*	*	*	*	*		
Concentric						*	*
magneto ignition	*	*	*	*	*	*	
capacitor ignition							*
12 volt electrics			*	*	*	*	*
wider forks			*	*	*	*	*
3/8 in. rear chain			*	*	*	*	*
seat hump							*

Nomad

Feature	'58	'59	'60
twin carbs	*	*	*
magneto ignition	*	*	*
alternator	*	*	*
77 frame	*	*	*
21 in. front	*	*	*
88 Nomad			*
88 with coil			*

745 cc MX models

Feature	'63	'64	'65	'66	'67	'68
Atlas MX	*	*				
N15CS'N'			*	*	*	*
N15CS						*
AMC frame	*	*	*	*	*	*
Norton forks	*	*	*	*	*	*
Norton hubs	*	*	*	*	*	*
twin carbs	*	*	*	*	*	*

745 cc Trail Models

Feature	'67	'68
P11	*	
P11A		*
Ranger		*
Concentrics	*	*
G85CS frame	*	*
AMC forks	*	*
AMC hubs	*	*
waist exhaust	*	
low exhaust		*

G15/33 series

Years	'65	'66	'67	'68	'69
G15/33 listed	*	*	*		
G15Mk2 listed				*	*
G15CSR listed	*	*	*	*	*
G15CS listed			*	*	*
33CSR listed	*	*	*		

Commando
Build periods

745 cc machines	
20M3	4.68-2.69
Fastback	3.69-8.70
Fastback II	9.70-12.70
Fastback III	1.71-12.71
Fastback IV	1.72-3.73
R	3.69-10.69
S	3.69-6.70
Fastback LR	4.71-12.71
Fastback LR IV	1.72-3.73
Roadster	3.70-12.70
Roadster II	1.71-12.71
Roadster IV	1.72-2.73
Roadster V	3.73-10.73
SS	3.71-10.71
Hi-Rider	5.71-12.71
Hi-Rider IV	1.72-2.73
Hi-Rider V	3.73-10.73
Interstate	1.72-2.73
Interstate V	3.73-10.73
Production racer	4.71-10.73

829 cc machines	
Roadster 1	4.73-12.73
Roadster 1A	9.73-2.75
Roadster 2A	1.74-2.75
Roadster 3	2.75-10.77
Interstate 1	4.73-12.73
Interstate 1A	9.73-2.75
Interstate 2A	1.74-2.75
Interstate 3	2.75-10.77
Hi-Rider 1	4.73-12.73
Hi-Rider 2	1.74-2.75
Hi-Rider 3	1975
JPR	11.73-2.75

20M3, Fastback and LR

Feature	'68	'69	'70	'71	'72	'73
t/case points		*	*	*	*	*
cartridge filter					*	*
rear breather pipe					*	*
Combat engine					*	
tubular silencer	*	*				
reverse-cone silencers			*	*	*	*
slimline forks				*	*	*
8 in. 2LS front brake	*	*	*	*		
disc front brake					*	*
dualseat ears	*	*	*	*	*	*
right side cover				*	*	*
tail unit	*	*	*	*	*	*
built-in bar switches				*	*	*

S

Feature	'69	'70
t/case points	*	*
waist exhausts	*	*
reverse-cone silencer	*	*
slimline forks	*	*
right side panel	*	*

Production Racer

Feature	'71	'72	'73
cockpit fairing	*	*	*
clip-ons/rearsets	*	*	*
disc front brake	*	*	*

Hi-Rider

Feature	'71	'72	'73
t/case points	*	*	*
cartridge oil filter		*	*
rear breather pipe		*	*
reverse-cone silencer	*	*	*
slimline forks	*	*	*
8 in. 2LS front brake	*	*	*
small tank	*	*	*
humped seat	*	*	*
high bars	*	*	*
turn signal option			*

R

Feature	'69
no tail unit	*
small tank	*
dualseat	*

SS

Feature	'71
waist exhaust each side	*
reverse-cone silencer	*
undershield	*
braced handlebars	*
small tank	*

Roadster

Feature	'70	'71	'72	'73
t/case points	*	*	*	*
cartridge oil filter			*	*
rear breather pipe			*	*
Combat engine			*	
low exhausts	*	*	*	*
reverse-cone silencer	*	*	*	*
slimline forks	*	*	*	*
8 in. 2LS front brake	*	*		
disc front brake			*	*
pleated seat top	*	*	*	
right side panel	*	*	*	*
built-in bar switches		*	*	*
turn signal option				*

Interstate

Feature	'72	'73
t/case points	*	*
cartridge oil filter	*	*
rear breather pipe	*	*
Combat engine	*	
shallow-taper silencer	*	*
slimline forks	*	*
disc front brake	*	*
large tank	*	*
right side panel	*	*
built-in bar switches	*	*
turn signals	*	*

829 cc Roadster & Interstate

Feature	'73	'74	'75	'76	'77
new cylinder block	*	*	*	*	*
t/case inspection plug			*	*	*
short-stroke engine (Roadster)			*		
exhaust balance pipe	*	*	*	*	*
reverse-cone silencer (Roadster)	*				
shallow-taper silencer (Inter)	*				
'black cap' silencer		*	*	*	*
electric start			*	*	*
chaincase screws			*	*	*
left foot gear pedal			*	*	*
vernier Isolastics			*	*	*
plastic air box		*	*	*	*
disc front brake	*	*	*	*	*
front caliper on left			*	*	*
disc rear brake			*	*	*
warning lamp console			*	*	*
pleated seat top		*	*	*	*

829 cc Hi-Rider

Feature	'73	'74	'75
new cylinder block	*	*	*
exhaust balance pipe	*	*	*
reverse-cone silencer	*	*	*
disc front brake	*	*	*
humped seat	*	*	*
electric start			*
left foot gear pedal			*

John Player Norton

Feature	'74
listed	*

Jubilee

Feature	'59	'60	'61	'62	'63	'64	'65	'66
de luxe listed	*	*	*	*	*			
standard listed			*	*	*	*	*	*
light forks	*	*	*	*	*	*	*	*
6 in. brakes	*	*	*	*	*	*	*	*
18 in. wheels	*	*	*	*	*	*	*	*
flat handlebars						*	*	*
wider rear no. plate						*	*	*

Navigator

Feature	'61	'62	'63	'64	'65
de luxe listed	*	*	*		
standard listed	*	*	*	*	*
Roadholder forks	*	*	*	*	*
8 in. front brake	*	*	*	*	*
19 in. front wheel	*	*	*	*	*
flat handlebars				*	*
wider rear no. plate				*	*

Electra

Feature	'63	'64	'65
electric start	*	*	*
Roadholder forks	*	*	*
8 in. front brake	*	*	*
7 in. rear brake	*	*	*
19 in. front wheel	*	*	*
12 volt electrics	*	*	*
turn signals	*	*	*
flat handlebars		*	*
wider rear no. plate		*	*

Colour notes

These are given to aid identification and, thus, are outlines rather than the full details, as in *Norton Twin Restoration.* Detail parts should be in black or to match the machine's colour, while the wheel rims may be black, chrome-plated with painted centres, or simply chrome-plated. Headlamp shells were usually painted, but could be plated, and some mudguards were in light alloy or stainless steel. The data should assist when viewing a machine, as an incorrect colour indicates either a change of part or a repaint. This may not matter, but it is as well to know.

Manx
1946-63	all black, tank silver

International
1946-52	all black, tank silver
1953-54	all grey, tank chrome with grey panels
1955-58	as 1953, round tank badges

16H
1945-51	all black, tank chrome with silver panels
1951-54	all black, tank silver

Big 4
1947-51	all black, tank chrome with silver panels
1951-54	all black, tank silver

18
1945-51	all black, tank chrome with silver panels
1951-52	all black, tank silver
1953-54	all black, tank chrome with silver panels

ES2
1947-51	all black, tank chrome with silver panels
1951-52	all black, tank silver
1953-54	all black, tank chrome with silver panels
1955-56	all black, tank chrome with silver panels and round badges
1957-58	all black, tank silver with chrome panels and round badges
1959	all forest green, tank with chrome panels and round badges
1960	as 1959, option of chrome mudguards
1961-62	two-tone green with dove grey for lower tank and mud guards only, long tank badges, option of chrome mudguards
1963	two-tone black with off-white for lower tank and mud guards only, long tank badges, option of chrome mudguards
1965	all black, tank silver with round badges
1966	all black, tank silver with transfers

19
1955-56	all black, tank chrome with silver panels and round badges

1957-58	all black, tank silver with chrome panels and round badges

50

1956	all black, tank chrome with silver panels and round badges
1957-58	all black, tank silver with chrome panels and round badges
1959	all forest green, tank with chrome panels and round badges
1960	as 1959, option of chrome mudguards
1961-62	two-tone black with dove grey for lower tank and mud guards only, long tank badges, optionof chrome mudguards
1963	two-tone black with off-white for lower tank and mud guards only, long tank badges, optionof chrome mudguards
1965	all black, tank silver with round badges
1966	all black, tank silver with transfers

500T

1949-54	all black, tank dull chrome with silver panel

Model 7

1949-51	all black, tank chrome with silver panels
1952	all black, tank silver
1953-54	all black, tank chrome with silver panels
1955	as 1953, round tank badges

77

1957-58	all grey, tank with chrome side panels and round badges

88

1952-54	all grey, tank chrome with grey panels
1955-56	as 1952, round tank badges
1957-58	all grey, tank grey with chrome panels and round badges
1959	all grey, blue or red, tank to match with chrome panels and round badges; option of chrome mudguards
1960	two-tone in red, grey or black with dove grey, long tank badges; option of chrome mudguards
1961-62	two-tone in green and dove grey, long tank badges; option of chrome mudguards
1963	two-tone in green and off-white, long tank badges

88 de luxe

1960	two-tone in red, grey, blue or forest green with dove grey, long tank badges
1961-62	two-tone in red and dove grey, long tank badges

88SS

1961-62	two-tone in green and dove grey, long tank badges; option of chrome mudguards
1963	two-tone in black and silver, long tank badges; option of chrome mudguards
1964-66	two-tone in black and silver, long tank badges, chrome mudguards

99

1956	all grey, tank chrome with grey panels and round badges
1957-58	all grey, tank grey with chrome panels and round badges
1959	all grey, blue or red, tank to match with chrome panels and round badges; option of chrome mudguards

1960	two-tone in red, grey or black with dove grey, long tank badges; option of chrome mudguards
1961-62	two-tone in grey and dove grey, long tank badges; option of chrome mudguards

99 de luxe

1960	two-tone in red, grey, blue or forest green with dove grey, long tank badges
1961-62	two-tone in blue and dove grey, long tank badges

99SS

1961-62	two-tone in grey and dove grey, long tank badges; option of chrome mudguards

650

1961	two-tone in grey and dove grey, long tank badges; option of chrome mudguards
1962	all grey, long tank badges; option of chrome mudguards
1963	two-tone in black with blue tank and mudguards, long tank badges

650 de luxe

1962	two-tone in blue and dove grey, long tank badges

650SS

1962-63	black, tank silver with long badges; option of chrome mudguards
1964-68	black, tank silver with long badges, chrome mudguards

Mercury

1969	black, tank silver; mud-guards, oil tank, chaincase and battery cover blue
1970	black, silver tank, chrome mudguards

Atlas

1962	black, tank silver, long badges chrome mudguards
1963	black, tank red, long badges, chrome mudguards
1964	black, tank red or black, long badges, chrome mudguards
1965	black, tank cherry red, long badges, chrome mudguards
1966	black, tank burgundy, long badges, chrome mudguards
1967-68	black, tank cherry red, long badges, chrome mudguards

Nomad

1958-60	black, alloy mudguards, red tank with chrome panels

Atlas MX

1964	black, silver petrol tank, oil tank and battery cover, chrome mudguards
1968	black, red tank, chrome mudguards

Trail

1967-68	black, tank red with round badges, chrome mudguards
1968	Ranger black with red tank and side covers, tank transfers, chrome mudguards

Commando

All models have a black frame, either stainless or chrome mudguards and a variety of colours for the petrol tank, oil tank, side covers and tail unit. See *Norton Twin Restoration* for full details of all these items. Below are listed the colours that were offered for each model and year.

Fastback

1969	green, red or silver
1970	as 1969 plus yellow, blue and bronze
1971-72	red, green, blue or bronze

Fastback LR
1971-72   red or green

R and S
1969-70   red or blue
1970   S as Fastback

Roadster
1970   red, green, silver, yellow, blue or bronze
1971-72   black, red, yellow, orange, blue, bronze or purple
1973   yellow, black or blue

SS
1971   yellow or tangerine

Hi-Rider
1971-72   yellow or tangerine
1973   yellow, tangerine or black

Interstate
1972   black, blue or red
1973   black or blue

Production racer
1971-73   yellow

850 Roadster
1973   bronze, blue, black or red
1974   as 1973 or white
1975-77   black, red or white

850 Interstate
1973-74   black or blue
1975-77   black, red or silver

850 Hi-Rider
1973   black
1974   tangerine
1975   black

John Player Norton
1974   white

Jubilee de luxe
1959-60   two-tone in red, green or blue with dove grey
1961-62   two-tone in blue and dove grey
1963   two-tone in blue and dove grey, or in black and off-white

Jubilee standard
1961-62   two-tone in red and dove grey
1963   two-tone in red and dove grey, or in burgundy and black; option of chrome mud guards
1964-66   two-tone in burgundy and black

Navigator de luxe
1961-63   two-tone in black and dove grey

Navigator standard
1961   two-tone in blue and dove grey
1962   two-tone in blue and dove grey; option of chrome mudguards
1963   two-tone in blue and dove grey, or in blue and black; option of chrome mudguards
1964-65   two-tone in blue and black

Electra
1963   black, tank silver; option of chrome mudguards
1964-65   black, tank silver, chrome mudguards

Clubs, spares and data sources

An important aspect of motorcycling is knowing where to get parts and information for your machine. Spares and services are essential to all owners at some time or other, and a list of people and firms who can help can be very useful in times of stress. The owner's club can help with this, so it is well worth joining, regardless of where you live, as it will provide addresses and contacts which often can be just what is needed.

To locate the club and dealers, use one or more of the current motorcycle magazines. Hunt around your local newsagent or book shop for titles such as the weekly *Motor Cycle News*, although for a Norton you are likely to be better off with magazines such as *Classic Bike, Classic Motor Cycle, Classic Mechanics, Old Bike Mart* or *British Bike Magazine*. Within their pages you will find the contact addresses for the Norton Owner's club plus advertisements for services and parts. *Classic Bike* publishes a supplier guide each year in their October issue, and this can be a great help.

You may well ask why the addresses are not here, and the answer is the time scale of book production and the period a book's print run stays on sale. A magazine can print a correction or change in its next issue, but only one copy of a book is bought by most people. Thus, what happens is that soon after the book is published, the club secretary either resigns or moves house and the suppliers change addresses or telephone numbers. The result tends to be chaos, so it is best if you find the addresses you need from the above sources.

You need to know about the magazines, anyway, as they respond to changes in the market in a way that is impossible in a book. This is especially important on the matter of prices, which are also not included here, as they go out of date even faster than club secretaries. You should be using the small ads to check out values and asking prices well before you go out to shop, as this is the way to get good value. Make full use of the magazines in this way as well as for tracking down things you need.

Data sources

These are the books, parts lists and manuals. The Norton owner is fortunate in having an ample supply of literature available which does make ownership easier. The books are listed with a note as to the author and publisher.

Norton Twins by Roy Bacon, published by Osprey

A history of the postwar twins which concentrates on the road machines, but includes a chapter on the Wankel and Wulf. It includes information on the use of the machines in competition with a reference to the Cosworth models. The detailed appendices are a strong feature and include specifications, engine and frame numbers, recognition details, colours, prices and carburettor settings.

Norton Twin Restoration by Roy Bacon, published by Osprey

A guide for restoration and parts identification which, thus, includes the development history of the twins from 1949 to 1977. The very extensive appendices have been highly praised by reviewers. This is the book you need to turn a basket case into a concours winner.

Norton Singles by Roy Bacon, published by Osprey

A history that covers the marque from its earliest days to the end of the singles line.

Covers all single-cylinder models and has the same detailed appendices as the twins.

Norton Story by Bob Holliday, published by Patrick Stephens

A full marque history presented as a chronological story with nearly 80 photographs. Covers the history fully.

The Unapproachable Norton by Bob Holliday, published by Beaulieu

Pictorial history of the marque with a heavy concentration on road racing.

Pictorial History of Norton Motorcycles by Jim Reynolds, published by Temple Press

Another history in pictures with extensive captions and a lead into each period. Runs from the earliest days to 1958.

Manx Norton by Mick Walker, published by Aston Publications

The in-depth story of the most famous of all road racing motorcycles, covering the machines, the people involved, the exploits and the background with numerous illustrations.

British Motor Cycles since 1950 - volume 3 by Steve Wilson, published by Patrick Stephens

One in a series and with the bulk of the volume devoted to Norton, but also covers from Greeves to Norman via Hesketh, Indian and James.

Norton by Dennis Howard, published by Ballantyne Books

A USA paperback that is seldom seen in the UK, but is worth having.

Norton From 1946 by Cyril Ayton, published by Bay View Books

Reprints of road tests and other material from the magazines of 1946 to 1968.

Norton Motorcycles 1928 to 1955, published by Bruce Main-Smith

A booklet first published by *Motor Cycling* and packed with information on the Norton models of the years given. Handy if you have one.

The First Knocker Norton Scene by Bruce Main-Smith

Written by, photographed for, and published in 1979 by B M-S in his Scene book series. Includes some 133 pictures in 64 pages, all taken of machines as they were in 1976-78 and ranging from the early Moore engine to the late Carroll. Useful reference material.

Norton Commando - all models by Roy Bacon, published by Niton Publishing

A Motorcycle Monograph covering this one model in all its many forms from start to finish. Well illustrated.

Norton Dominator Twins - 1949-1970 by Roy Bacon, published by Niton Publishing

A Motorcycle Monograph that runs from the first Model 7 to the last Featherbed twin and includes the off-road models. Ample pictures.

Manx Norton Super Profile by Cyril Ayton, published by Haynes

Brief history of the one model in usual format for this series, giving details of development and competition use plus a photo gallery in colour as well as black and white.

International Norton Super Profile by Cyril Ayton, published by Haynes

Brief history, as above, of these models which had a special place in Norton history.

Norton Commando Super Profile by Jeff Clew, published by Haynes

History of the last model built in large numbers by the firm.

Norton by E.M. Franks, published by Pearson.

Long out of print, but one in a series written by the service managers of the firms and bound in red covers. Very good coverage from 1932 on and still to be found in various editions at autojumbles.

The Book of the Norton Dominator Twins by W.C. Haycroft, published by Pitman

Covers the twins with many editions produced, but not as deep or as highly regarded as the Pearson series. For all that, a handy publication to have on the shelf.

The Book of the Norton by W.C. Haycroft, published by Pitman

Covers the singles in the same manner as the first book.

Norton Service & Overhaul Manual by F.W. Neill, published by Lodgemark Press

In effect, this is two Norton workshop manuals printed as one book. It is not always easy to follow, but the information is there if you take the trouble to find it.

Commando Service Notes, published by the Norton Owner's Club

If you run a Commando then you should have this book. It covers the model in depth and without mercy, so all the faults and problems are investigated and solutions given. Essential reading.

Norton Tuning by Paul Dunstall, published by Lodgemark Press

Paul was THE name in Norton twin tuning in the 1960s, and this is the book you need if you wish to tune your engine. This is where you start.

Haynes and Clymer manuals, which cover many of the Norton models in their own special ways. Useful, but make sure that the one you use is relevant to your model.

Thanks to the machines' popularity, most books on the post-war British motorcycle scene contain references to Norton to some extent. Some of these books are of a more general nature, while others look at specific fields of the sport. Most specialist motor cycle book dealers will be happy to advise on these and their Norton content.

For maintenance and workshop manuals, Norton produced material which will enable the owner to carry out the tasks needed to keep the machine in good condition. The content of these books varied from model to model and year to year, but should be adequate for normal purposes. Many are still to be found at autojumbles or swop meets, but if not, reprints are available.

Parts lists for the postwar era are also available from the same sources, there being one list for singles and another for twins in most cases. There may be variations on this, but the dealers in such material can usually supply the correct item for any model, either as originals or photocopies. For all such material, use the adverts in the magazines and you will soon locate what you need.